# One Eyed Jack

## THE UNCOVERED MYSTERY OF CLAM RIVER

4/30/14

Louise

Read & Enjoy

### BY RC ROBOTHAM

Ron Robotham

ISBN: 1480028320
ISBN-13: 9781480028326

Library of Congress Control Number: 2012918627
CreateSpace Independent Publishing Platform
North Charleston, South Carolina

# Dedication

*This book is dedicated to the late Mary Kay McDuffie.*
*She loved Torch Lake and therefore, also Clam River.*
*I thank Mary Kay for her help and encouragement*
*while doing research for my writing.*
*I grieve that her health struggle with ALS ended her*
*life before I could share this publication with her.*

# Introduction

*Why, oh why? Why would a guy*

*Want to tell the world at this late date*

*Of a time long ago, growing up by the lake?*

*The water does pass and like life goes*

*As surely as sunshine, it flows and it flows.*

*So better yet to the river I go*

*To share my search for who I am*

*And how I found a part of that self*

*In a store and on a porch by the River Clam.*

Recently, I was walking with my dog along our regular route that takes us out for a distance of about two miles. As one wise dog owner mentioned, "The number one thing my dog has taught me is to always be ready to take a walk." That's good advice for all of us.

Part of our walking course took us past an undeveloped area. There the grass, weeds, and sumac grew in a tangle. We walked past that area without anything abnormal happening, but I looked into the weeds and saw a cat crouched down. I immediately wondered whether it would jump my dog or whether my dog would see it and try to chase it, dragging me along. It appeared to be a feral cat, or at least it looked incredibly unkempt. Let me note here that I do like cats. Admittedly, I prefer dogs, but I do not hate cats in any way. But still, this cat had not just surprised and scared me a bit: this was also the ugliest cat I had ever seen. The cat was scruffy and dirty and, most distinctively, had only one eye. The lost eye, furthermore, had not healed well, and I guessed it was the result of the cat's coming out on the wrong end of a street fight.

I muttered, "One-Eyed Jack!" Instead of reacting with a scream or jumping away, I laughed. "One-Eyed Jack!" I hadn't thought of that for years. Incidentally, my half-blind nearly deaf dog never saw the cat or even sensed its presence, and we just continued on down the road. But I want to tell you a story about One-Eyed Jack—not this one but another one from over forty years ago. One-Eyed Jack became a symbol for me of who I was at a younger time, when I was just "working on mysteries without any clues," to quote an old song lyric.

A lot of these "mysteries" did not become clearer when viewed down the road. As I have grown older, I have tried for my family's sake to gather and record significant events that, together, have made my life what it is. I've reflected on how I developed certain attitudes and, especially, how I came to value diversity.

One thing I have claimed about myself over the years is that I have always loved people. I chose not to pursue engineering as a career. It appeared to be a lonely job in a laboratory. Instead, I have been a teacher, a camp manager, a transitional-housing provider, and I have interacted with people from many walks and talks of life. I have loved it and still do. Some say I inherited it from my gregarious father, but there is more to it that I would like to share.

I have often given my father credit not only for granting me my "gift of gab" but also for showing me that all people have value and can be appreciated for their characteristics or skills. Once I saw a truck driver on a busy Manhattan four-lane pull up slowly and wait for the light ahead to stop the traffic coming toward him. He quickly shifted into reverse and whipped that trailer perfectly into an alley that could not have had more than two feet clearance on a side. He did it so fast, he disappeared into the alley by the time the light changed and traffic resumed. Now there was a skill I could admire.

On the farm, I grew up with numerous tractors and pieces of equipment. I learned to drive and appreciate each of them along with the specific work they could do. Once I had a man do some work for me with his tractor and backhoe. I was amazed as I watched him work with such ease and grace. I watched him dig carefully around buried water pipes and concealed, unprotected, underground wires. He never touched a wire. I often commented, "He could pick up a baby with that tool!" I respected him for that skill I did not possess.

As I grew, I learned through my work experiences to appreciate and respect all types of people. We sold produce, and I learned to help satisfy even the fussiest customers. After working on the farm, I worked two summers at a grocery store in a resort area. All kinds of people came through our store – the fun and the grumpy and the snotty and the kind. Resort areas are full of stereotype people—people of class and money, who own cottages, belong to yacht clubs, and expect local boys who work in the stores to carry their groceries to their boats without providing any kind of tip. I learned from them all and tried to enjoy the experience instead of dwelling on their negative traits.

That brings me back to my story about One-Eyed Jack. This story took place in those couple of years after high school when I worked summers at a store. The story and characters are all fictional; many characters and events have roots in real people and circumstances, but all have been protected and their situations altered. If there is any resemblance to actual happenings, it is only accidental. This story is a compilation of events and feelings that help me express how I began to practice diversity in my life, the same diversity I celebrate and seek today.


For now, settle back and let me tell you a story,

# 1 – The Porch

*Can one's life change in just one fateful night?*

*Can a life get its meaning?*

*Can all seem suddenly right?*

*No, not for me. I've stumbled along.*

*To walk on a porch?*

*To sing a good song?*

*To hear a strange voice at an equally strange time?*

*And to respond to an invite?*

*These all have been mine.*

I was not sure if I was too scared to realize I was soaked and standing in the rain or if I was too wet, miserable, and exhausted from pushing to realize I was scared. Whichever it was, I heard the voice speak again.

"Park that thing and come up on the porch and get dry."

Ghosts don't talk that clearly, or so I had read somewhere. I crossed the road, kicked out the stand, and parked the bike. Instinctively, I took out the key. I had no real reason to. I surely was not worried that someone would steal it, especially a ghost; besides, the bike didn't even run.

I had never been this close to the haunted cottage we called, colloquially, the Jack Shack. Many people named their cottages similarly to how they might name their boats. A boat might be named the *Mary II* or *My Retirement* or any of a long list of creative and not-so-creative names. The names of cottages are very similar and include such things as The Roast and Sunset Cove. But "The Jack Shack" had evolved from a faded name on an extremely rusted mailbox that sat askew on a post by the walk leading to the cottage or shack or whatever one might call this place. This sign was old and had obviously been unaltered for many years. We could not read much except *The* at the beginning; then there was a space, and *ack* was at the end. So someone must have concluded it used to say *The Shack*. No one seemed concerned with the big space between *The* and *ack*, and obviously none of us took much of our teen curiosity to figure out an alternative. So we put the mailbox and the sign together and adopted "The Jack Shack," which we used to refer to it if we were feeling kind, though we would call it "The Haunted Shack" if we wanted to tell a scarier story. The former name sounded catchy and kind of ran off your tongue in a quick snap—"The Jack Shack!"—sort of like the title to a song.

At that moment, I couldn't have cared less about the name or the haunting, and I stepped carefully up on the porch out of the downpour. I took off my glasses, took out my handkerchief, and cleared the glasses of raindrops. I looked around. I was always one to take in lots of details, and I always joked that it came from my father's admonition at a very young age to "always keep your eyes open for deer." I think looking for deer was his biggest joy, and we spent a lot of my childhood in that pursuit.

Along with being unfamiliar with the place, it was dark, so I stepped carefully up the three short steps. There was no porch light at the door, but light came from a larger window to my left in front of which were a couple of old rockers. As my eyes adjusted, I noticed the farthest rocker was occupied, and the voice spoke again.

"Come. Sit a spell." He beckoned me to the other well-worn rocker; as I sat down in it, it surprised me as it rocked backward. The man chuckled.

"Don't worry," he said and reached over and threw me a towel. It was a welcomed offer, for I was dripping wet. This was long before the age of helmets, and my long hair dripped. I mumbled thanks and continued to dry off. The only sound was the loud rattle of the rain on the roof. The amount of noise led me to wonder if the roof or at least the part of the roof over the porch might be metal. I dried myself. The chairs rocked, and the rain continued to drum on the roof. We sat.

After a long pause, I managed to say, "Sorry to get the cushions wet!" and all I got in response was a "naw" or some kind of snort from the man. We continued rocking and listening to the rain.

As I said earlier, the light inside seemed to come from a lamp sitting on a table in an interior room. It seemed very adequate, even bright enough to read by, and I was curious about the two chairs sitting at just the right angle to catch that light. I noticed a small stand or stool or maybe just a box sitting on the floor between us with a magazine or two on it. With two chairs I assumed there must be a wife, but I didn't ask.

Because we sat at the end of the porch away from the road, it did dawn on me why most people would think this place was abandoned. There was no light on the road side of it, and I could only wonder whether there was a room there. My mind wandered. There was another odd thing about the porch that I noted. The porch ran along the long dimension of the cabin for sure, but it was not parallel to the road and not looking out on the lake but was at a funny angle. The cabin sat at more of a slant to the road with big bushes on that side. No one would notice a light on in the back unless he or she stopped and came down along and then up on the porch, as I had tonight. With no porch light and no yard light on a pole, the place seemed very dark and eerie.

We sat, and neither one of us spoke for some time. I'm not usually the quiet type, again, having certainly learned a thing or two from my gregarious father. Usually I had the ability to pick up a conversation with most anyone. But tonight we just sat in the silence. In the dark I couldn't see much, but I noticed the chairs were as old and worn as the cottage itself. There did not seem to be a vehicle or a garage, but I could tell there were some smaller buildings off the end of the porch toward the lake.

The waves of the lake were the first sounds I began to hear as the rain slowed. The breeze had picked up as the rain moved off to the east, the coolness of the lake almost giving me, rain-soaked, a chill. The breeze rustled the bushes, and one limb scraped sharply on the house or maybe the roof, and again I was startled and jumped. I certainly felt nervous. I held and folded and unfolded the towel in my lap. The silence was filling with more night sounds as the rain slowed to a mere dripping from the trees.

The towel—now there was a mystery in and of itself. Obviously, he had the towel with him. Did he just keep a towel by his chair all the time? Was he waiting for me all the time? Why would he have expected me to stop, for I never had before?

Or did he step inside, grab the towel, and sit down before I made it to the porch?

Although I had gathered a lot of information as to the mystery of this "haunted" cottage, the man was not offering any conversation to help me further. His quietness unsettled me almost as much as my previous fear of haunting ghosts had. He did reach down a couple times and light those old kitchen-type matches to relight his pipe. I have always liked the smell of the pipe. I also assigned a sage like wisdom to an old man sitting and slowly smoking a pipe. I sort of had a vision of the wise professor type with students (or, in this case, student) sitting and breathing in his wise words and aromatic pipe. But he wasn't teaching me this time; we just sat.

I noticed the eaves had stopped dripping, so I began uneasily to plan my leaving. I folded the towel again and noticed it was dirty from wiping my muddy arms and legs. Finally I muttered, "Thank you for the towel, but it is pretty dirty."

"No big problem," the man gently replied. I couldn't help but relax, for his voice was soothing. I could not put my finger on why, but it just felt right.

I rose from the chair, though not very easily—it was more like I'd crawled out of it. "I'd better go. It has stopped." I fumbled uncomfortably with the towel, not sure whether to hand it to him or put it on the chair or do something else.

"You'd better take that towel and wipe off your bike." With that, the man of few words sort of said good-bye; but did he?

"Thanks again." One thought crossed my mind: I should apologize for the years of teenage jokes and accusations I'd made about this scary place. Instead, though, I just stammered, "See you again sometime," and I walked back to my bike. My dominant thought was "Man, what a blunderbuss with words I am!"

I got to my bike and dried off the seat and handlebars. Again instinctively, I took out the key and put it in the ignition. I don't know why I thought to try to start it again, for it wasn't running before and now it had been sitting out in the rain for all this time. How long had it been, anyway, I wondered. I had certainly lost all track of time. I turned the key, pushed up the kickstand, and turned the gas on the right handle grip a couple times like I always did. Then I pushed the kick-starter; nothing happened. I pushed it again, and to my surprise it started. Now I jumped on, but what about the towel? I stuffed it in the saddlebag, promising myself to wash and return it.

I shifted into gear and rode off with my mind racing. The most prominent thought now was that I wanted to know more about this mysterious, kind, quiet man I had met tonight. Then it dawned on me, as I slowed for the stop sign under that second street light at the main road, that he had never told me his name.

That was all the more reason to return the towel soon, I thought, and that thought rattled in my head all the way home.

# 2 - Questioning

*Puzzles and mysteries swirl in my head.*

*To have talked to a ghost? Surely not dead!*

*Who was he? And more so, why me?*

*Of all the nights? Of all the days?*

*Of all the lights? Of all the ways?*

*On the banks of the Clam where I came to be,*

*Who was he? And more so, why me?*


"You're quiet and seem full of thought," my dad said.

"Yeah, that is true."

"How is work at the ol' River Clam?" My dad tried to chide me out of my quietness.

"Sure is different than what we used to do up on the farm. I do like being around so many people, though, all so different and interesting."

My dad smiled and kidded me in his usual way about my girl-friends. "Yeah, I bet you are suffering with all those pretty resort girls in and out of the store!"

"Oh, Dad!" Then I agreed: "However, that is true!" We both laughed. "I think I have gotten to think more and observe more about other people than I had ever done before this."

"Yep, I think you are growing up, Son. Say, do you want more cookies or something more for snack? Your mom always has great goodies around."

"No, thanks."

My dad's look seemed to get a bit introspective, which I don't particularly remember seeing often. He sat there looking past me out the window of our kitchen. This was a new house for all of us. My parents had just moved here off the farm in the spring, not long before I got home from college. All of us were adjusting to the change, which I can only imagine was more upsetting for them than it was for me because I had been away from home and living the adventure of growing up on my own.

He spoke slowly. "I've always liked people, too. Maybe that's why farming seemed kind of lonely. Most of the work we did was pretty much by yourself; even when there were others working, they were working in some other place on the farm on some other task, also alone. I think we are a bit alike that way."

It got kind of quiet, which, as I mentioned earlier, was odd for my father, who was a notoriously good talker. He eventually spoke up again. "Are you still thinking hard about something? I'm all ears!"

That was a new one for our relationship. Maybe I was growing and appreciating my dad more, especially after he'd dealt
with his recent struggles with the farm and all. I laughed, not
rudely, mind you, but I couldn't help it because just then I had
an image of my dad's head as two big ears. I began to choose my
words carefully.

"Did you ever meet any of the folks who lived along the road
coming up to the Clam River Bridge? You know, there are two or
three cottages along there that all must be summer places 'cause I
never see much action at them."

"No. I don't know any of those folk. Why?"

"Oh, just wondering. Remember that oldest cottage in the
middle especially looks abandoned? The kids always joked about it
being haunted! Did you ever see anyone around there?"

"Not that I can recall. Why? Did you see a ghost there?"

We laughed. My dad laughed a lot. I guess I was learning to
appreciate more and more about him. Many people remember him
as a guy with a smile or a good joke. That wasn't a bad legacy to
have.

He added, "You know, who you need to ask is Dan at the bar.
He knows everybody. I think he's lived all his life in this area. We
only moved up here six years—no, seven years ago now. Nope, he's
your man."

I agreed and added, "With the Tiger's game rained out, I'm
going to bed. There are too many long days, and having to close the
store makes them longer."

"Oh, you're young. You'll survive!"

"Good-night!" we chimed in unison and laughed again.

The next day I left for work a bit early. I decided to take my dad's advice and stop for a chat with Dan at the bar. I figured he wouldn't be too busy this early in the morning.

"Did you ever meet a man living in the old cottage up the road on the way down here?"

I was sure the owner of the bar and restaurant next to the store knew everybody as well as everything that went on around here. So I thought he would be a good person to ask. Unfortunately, I was always leery of Dan's answers because he had been proven to exaggerate or embellish his stories regularly. He and my father were good fishing buddies. They fished a lot together in the winter when the tourist season and the fruit season both ended. They would sit for hours on the lake fishing and telling tall tales.

There wasn't anyone else in the place at this time of the morning. It was too early for tourists, and I didn't have to be at work until eleven. Dan stopped his cleaning, poured himself some coffee, and came around to sit on a stool next to me.

"You seem so serious this morning, Captain."

Dan has always called me "Captain." It goes back to the first time we met. I was with my dad, and I was wearing one of those old fake captain's hats they sell to the tourists. That was at least five or six years ago, but he had never forgotten.

I didn't want to appear nosey or give away my mysterious experience of the night before, so I shrugged it off. "No, I'm just curious and making conversation."

Dan gave me a sideways glance and a smirk and sipped his coffee. I could tell he knew there was more to this than I was letting on, but he did not pry.

"When I was a kid, I remember a family lived there. They came up every summer, but I don't recall from where. The cottage didn't look as bad as it does now, but it was never a fancy place, very rustic. It just looked kind of worn and tired like it still does."

Dan took another sip, and I sat and listened as he went on.

"I remember a time my dad stopped and talked to the man there. I was a kid then, so that was thirty years ago at least. I recall my dad got some booze from him. It was after prohibition, so I don't understand or recall why. I sort of remember his comment on how he was related to the family who owned this place and the store next door. I think, back then, it was more like one big place, not two like it is now. You'll have to do some research, but I think the last name of those owners was 'Anderson.' I found an old sign once with that name, and someone here told me they owned this many years ago."

I listened closely. "Were there any children in the family?"

"I do not remember that at all, one way or the other. I just remember stopping there that one time and driving by it over the years. It was always dark and kind of lost, and many spoke of it as being haunted."

"Ha!" I laughed. "That is just like we do now! All the kids joke about how 'The Jack Shack' is haunted."

"The Jack Shack?" Dan said.

"Yes, it says 'Jack' on the old mailbox."

"True it is, and I do not recall whether that was their first or their last name."

I sat quietly thinking all this over as Dan finished his coffee. Eventually he said, "Why you askin' anyway?"

"Oh, nothing special," I muttered back.

He gave me another smirk and an "I don't believe that for a minute" look and headed to the back to get ready for the noon lunch crowd. He needed to get the grill turned on for big juicy burgers, which were his specialty and a local favorite. I slid down and noticed some pictures on the wall. I suppose they had always been there, but I had not taken notice until then. I saw that one of them was a boat—a steamer, I'd guess—either loading or unloading some smiling people. It was a pretty old photo, at least judging by the style of dress, and I could clearly see the name on the boat was *Mabel*.

The other picture was not quite as clear, but I could tell it was of this building. When I squinted in the dim light, I could see the big sign over the entrance read *Anderson's Store*. Curiously, it was a picture of a group of men, each with a mug or glass raised up like a toast. I wondered about the significance of this and was about to ask Dan when I realized it was two minutes to eleven and I needed to get my apron on for work. I hollered a hurried good-bye over my shoulder on my way out.

However, I could not stop thinking about all of this and almost bumped into a pretty young lady coming out the store door. "Oops, sorry," I said and then held the door. Afterward, I watched her closely as she walked off. "Wow!" and then "Get to work!" came from someone inside, and I noticed my boss glaring at me. I had just too many things to think about and distract me that day.

# 3 - Sunset

*I've never been one for mystery.*

*So who is this man, and what do I expect to see?*

*It is not like he's hiding there in his chair,*

*But I feel a strange draw to return to there.*

*Having moved to this area,*

*I have no grandfather who's close.*

*Maybe that's what I seek? Maybe that's what I lack?*

*So I walk in past the mailbox I notice again says Jack.*

*I don't know his name, nor does he mine.*

*What am I getting into this second time?*

I got off work early one evening later in the week. By *early* I mean around eight, so before it got dark, and I was curiously drawn to revisit the mysterious man on the porch. I stood beside my bike for a while, fussing with stuff in my saddlebags but mostly stalling. I was scared, curious, and cautious and at first wondered why I should go but then figured there was no reason not to stop. I started my bike and rode slowly over to the old cottage with the rusty mailbox hanging askew.

I stopped the bike and pushed it past the mailbox and behind the row of bushes. Was I embarrassed? Was I afraid of my pals kidding me about my conversations with a ghost?

I walked to the porch as I had done before. Now in the light, I could make out the scene better and confirm some of what I thought I had seen in the dark. The porch ran the length of the cottage, and I could see to the northwest a good view of the lake where the sun was preparing to set. There were no chairs at the near end of the porch, but there was a planter there with flowers draping over the edge. My mother and father loved flowers, so I was quick to notice one of my mom's favorites, pansies. Other than the bright pansies, everything looked—what was it Dan called it? Rustic? Well, maybe, but to me it just looked tired and worn.

There was a small window on that end of the porch, and it was dark. I couldn't tell for sure, but it seemed to have a dark curtain pulled shut. The other end was familiar as before, and I could already see the light streaming onto the porch from the lamp inside. This time I noticed there was a screen door on the entrance door. It was one of the older wooden styles. I noticed the screen was loose in the bottom-left corner. I didn't have time to question that because I soon heard his voice.

"Look who's here!" He said it with a lilt in his voice, and I thought I might have heard a hint of some accent. "Pull the other chair around."

It was then I realized I had not seen him when I stepped onto the porch because he had his chair turned away from me, directed out to the view of the lake. I followed his directions and pulled the chair I had used before up near his. The sun was setting, and the lake was, as always, alluring and beautiful. I just stood there for a minute soaking it in and letting all the dust of the day's work drift away. As before, a welcomed quiet came over me as I enjoyed the gentle sound of the waves lapping the beach and a small motor-boat putting away off in the distance. There was no breeze tonight, no branches coarsely scraping the roof, and no rain pounding, but the waves and a few birds chirping in the nearby trees gave this a peacefulness I had not taken time to notice in my hurry to grow up as a teenager.

"Sit," he directed.

I did as I was told, and I still held the cleaned towel in my lap, again not knowing what to do with it.

As before, although it was not nearly as uncomfortable as then, we sat in silence. I could see more now than during my first visit because there was more light, and I became determined that one shed was attached to the house on the lake side. The other shed was a bit larger and sat more to the back and north of the other and had some tools hanging on the side wall. I couldn't tell if they were there for use or for decoration. I observed to myself that the lawn did not look as if the tools had had much use lately.

Cottages on a lake often have docks and boats. As we sat and watched, I noticed that here there was neither. I noticed there were several fishing poles hanging on the side of the house just past the window. I couldn't tell if they were for use or for decoration either. The sun was sinking, and the colors were changing. But it was mostly silence between us as the minutes passed.

"Em and I sat out here many a night," he finally said, and I did not respond, some out of respect and mostly because I had nothing to say. Again I thought how it was so unlike me to be tongue-tied, but the captivating quiet of being there together seemed to fill and satisfy all my senses.

Again he spoke, though it seemed it was not especially to me but just to anyone listening.

"That's the advantage of being where we are, on the western edge of the time zone. Here we get great sunsets."

That comment meshed with my own science background, and I knew what he meant. I had been going to college in the Western Upper Peninsula even farther west than here. There the summer sun didn't set until way after ten. But his comment and that fact brought me back to considering the odd angular placement of this cottage. The road out front went straight from east to west, but this cottage was angled to the northwest and therefore provided a perfect view of those midsummer sunsets so far to the north. I wondered whether someone would build a cottage just to look at the sunsets. I thought I might actually ask him that...

Again he spoke. "Sunsets can be sad or delightful. They're the end of the day, the coming of darkness."

I was moved and responded, "You are quite the poet!"

It was then that he finally turned toward me, looked me deep in the eyes, and smiled. He had a wonderful smile, not the near-toothless grin of a haunting ghost. It made me feel even more comfortable.

"You like poetry?" he asked.

I shrugged. "I suppose."

He got up from his chair, and I realized it was the first time I had seen him standing. He got up slowly and rubbed the stiffness in his back. He was short and stout with wispy gray hair curled over his collar. I could not tell whether he was balding because he was wearing a worn Tiger baseball cap. It looked to be as old as I thought he was, but then again, to a young kid, everyone seems old. He was gone for several minutes, and I continued to survey the porch. I could still see more details in the evening's last light, and I strained to look around his now-empty chair; I saw a long planter along the porch end nearest the lake also holding flowers, but by now it was too dark to tell what they were. It again reminded me of my parents, who have lots of flowers planted every year around their house; even though my dad is not still farming, he loves to grow things. I jerked as I heard the screen door squeak.

He just said "here" and handed me a paper, and then he went over to his chair and resumed sitting in his now-familiar place. He glanced at the sun, still sinking over the lake, and reached down as usual, struck a match, and took a couple puffs of his pipe. "Go ahead and open it."

I opened the twice-folded paper and could tell it was worn, though I didn't know from what. Maybe it was something from long ago? Or maybe it was worn from many readings? Either way, I read what was written on it to myself:

> Em and I sat as the night drew nigh
> Watching the sunset and the day die.
> Some nights red and flashy;
> Others gray, threatening rain.
> Like life itself, when some days fly,
> And others stay just the same.
> We watch with sadness;

We watch with hope;
Sometimes we hold hands, and I am no dope.
I gave thanks daily for each loving chance.

I held the paper and read it again. We sat and drank in the silence, the cricket chorus our only distraction. Watching the sunset progress as it did, I felt it was like a holy moment and very reverently refolded the paper. He sat saying nothing and seemed far away. I figured from what I had read that this sunset reminded him of many other sunsets. Now this sunset was turning more blue and gray with red streaks. Then, almost in a flash, it took on an orange glow. The great orb showed half up and half down, sort of suspended and hanging. I am always amazed by how huge it looks right at the horizon, and somehow this setting tonight, the poem, and the old man magnified every feeling I think I had ever had. Then the sun was gone.

I did not want to break the silence as we sat for several minutes in the gathering darkness.

"Write many poems?" I asked.

After another pipe-lighting, he said, slowly, "Em liked 'em."

# 4 - "Em liked 'em"

*Who'd ever have thought*

*A Clam River bum would meet a poet*

*While sitting around just watching the sun?*

*Poetry is far from something I claim,*

*But this man's way leads me to a place.*

*It is hard to explain.*

*He shares, and I feel.*

*Now I read, and it's so real!*

*Wow, what an adventure the river brings,*

*And how I am celebrating all the new things.*

"Em liked 'em"—with that, the man of few words summed it all up.

I sensed somehow that Em was his wife and she had died. I wondered how long ago? I began to feel for his lonesomeness and deeply admired his friendly spirit in spite of it. I didn't know much about death or grief. Both of my parents and one set of my grandparents were still alive. My mother was from farther away, and her father died when she was in high school. I was not really close to my grandmother simply because she lived far away and we only saw her once or twice a year. I remember, sadly, that she eventually developed cancer and came to live with us. My mother cared for her constantly as she was dying. On the day she died, all my dad said to me was "You'd better go with the cherries and the truck over to the canning factory tonight." By the time I'd gotten home, her body was gone. The funeral was in Grand Rapids, and being in the middle of cherry harvest, I had to stay and run the farm. Like I said, I didn't know much of death or grief.

He seemed so calm and peaceful. But when he said "Em liked 'em," I could feel his longing for her, not me, to be there for the sunset. So again, why me? There I went over thinking it again. He explained how it was hard to return to this place. But he came back for a while each summer just to enjoy the sunsets and remember. I still did not know where else he lived and did not need to ask because I was so blessed he had shared.

I did not know what to say or do. So silence seemed the best action. As we sat I suddenly remembered the towel. I guess it was the excuse to break the uncomfortable silence, and I blurted out, "I brought back the towel. My mother made sure it was scrubbed clean from the mud."

"What? You didn't wash it yourself and made your mother do it?" In the darkness I could see his smile again; the light glistened off his teeth. There was another glistening on his cheek; I knew what that meant but had no clue what to say. "Thanks, I've got a plenty too many these days!" he said.

I also handed back the folded poem. "Thanks for sharing that," I said shyly and uncomfortably. A grunt was all I got back, and I announced, "Guess I'd better get going. I've got to clean up!"

"Got a date?"

"Yeah," I smiled.

"Bet she's pretty!"

I blubbered, "You bet," and I blushed and hoped he couldn't see it in the dark.

"You be sure and remember that. Be sure to tell her also!"

I nodded agreement and mumbled, "See you again," as I moved off the porch.

"I'd like that," I heard him say. I thought I should stop and acknowledge the comment but again was clueless as to what to say and so moved on toward my motorcycle instead.

Then I heard him speak again: "I don't even know your name!"

I stopped and turned back toward him. "Ron. Dan at the bar always calls me Captain, but Ron works best."

He waved a casual toss of his hand from his rocker. I left, pulled out of the drive, and headed toward home to shower before my much-anticipated date. What would I tell her about my new friend? "A friend?" I laughed to myself. "Next time I have got to learn his name, too!"

My girlfriend was a little miffed because I was a bit late. The movie had started, but it was exciting to be close again; soon the day's events seemed far away. We stopped after the movie at The Hot Spot on the edge of town, where pinball machines

clanged and Chubby Checker twisted on the jukebox. We chat-
ted about normal things. She too was working this summer at
a resort, as a nanny and a recreation director. Her job's tasks
varied, but she liked kids, and although wearing on her sometimes, she was happy with the work. It was a real treat for us to
have the same nights off and be able to get together. This was
our first date in over a week, and it felt good to snuggle close
and hold hands.

Unfortunately, like it was with so many jobs in resort country,
the hours were long for the both of us, and this night came to an
end all too soon. We both caught each other yawning and laughed.
We excused ourselves, and I took her home. She was so good to
be with, and we made plans for a dance coming up on Saturday.
We'd connect with our friends and drive to Traverse City together.
It would give us something good to look forward to through the
ninety-degree heat that was forecast for this week. Both of our
jobs were hot jobs, and even though we both worked on the lake, we
were never in the lake.

"So until Saturday," I said. "Oh, yes, you sure look beautiful
tonight!"

"Wow! What made you say that all of a sudden?"

"Oh, I was just reminded by…" I paused in mid thought. "I'll
tell you more about that sometime."

We held each other. "Can't wait until Saturday!" I said, and
then I got lost in those "kisses sweeter than wine."

After that I seemed to float off, although I actually drove the
several miles home. The night was dark with no moon and lots of

stars. I was amazed at the feelings I was learning about with my girlfriend. I also recalled the sunset and the old man. I'd enjoyed my visit to the cottage, and I wondered why. Why me? Why here? I began to think about several new feelings I had especially about talking with older people.

I got home and went up the stairs and through the kitchen. My folks were in bed, and I could hear my dad snoring. They always left a light on, and it illuminated my dad's favorite chair and a bookcase behind it. I guess I was noticing more lately or something. A book caught my eye. I reached over in the dimness, pulled it up to the light, and read the title: *The Poetry of Walt Whitman*. I pondered to myself: "Poetry twice in one night? This is too much!"

I reached up, turned off the light, and took the book to my bedroom. Even though my parents may have long been in bed, my mother said, "Good-night, Son."

I smiled at the familiar assurance. I said good-night and closed my bedroom door. Being away at college with no good-nights, as I had been this past year, I realized how easy it was to feel the "old" comfortable good-night routine, yet it was also uncomfortable. I was off into the "new" and wondered if I could ever look back.

I looked again at the book, sat down, and opened it. I feathered the pages. My thumb stopped the pages on some unnumbered place, and I read, "When lilacs last in dooryard bloom'd." I read on:

O ever returning spring, Trinity sure to me brings.

Lilac blooming perennial and drooping star in the west.

I thought of her I love.

I guess I was thinking of my evening warmth, but there seemed to be more. I continued to read and found myself struggling with understanding the form and meaning.

I woke with the sun streaming in through my window. I was still dressed, and the book of poetry was beside me, my finger still stuck in that spot.

# 5 - Names

*"What is in a name?" I think someone said.*

*Sounds like a poet; I'm sure he must be dead.*

*But this experience just resonates in me*

*Like a poem sometimes rhymes.*

*Suddenly this friendship through the names*

*Will push us ahead to far deeper gains.*

*Some names are fun and funny,*

*Others average with nothing sunny.*

*Today we discover there is a lot in a name,*

*And it will push us ahead—that is sure to be—*

*But also The Clam has richness in its own history.*

I turned to the chapter containing the poem I'd fallen asleep reading. The chapter was titled "Whitman and Lincoln." I sat and read the notes at the beginning of the chapter. Apparently, Whitman had always been quite politically outspoken and was especially critical of "politicians"—by which he meant any person working in the government long-term—or "the insiders," as some would call them. He was nonpartisan and criticized both parties for favoritism and nepotism. He longed for a "common man's president" and has an oft-quoted line where he expresses his wish for someone to come to the White House in working man's clothes from the farm or rural areas. He is credited with making that statement ten years before Lincoln's 1860 presidential win. He greatly supported and had high hopes for Lincoln during his period in office.

According to that book, the two men never met but surely knew of each other. Whitman also lived in Washington, and thus they both recalled, in journals, having seen each other in passing. Historians generally agree that Lincoln and Whitman admired and respected each other equally but had never exchanged views.

The first poem I had read about the lilacs was one of the grief poems Whitman wrote after Lincoln's death. "When Lilacs Last in the Dooryard Bloom'd" refers to Lincoln's death being in the spring and how every spring reminds Whitman of his sadness about it.

The next poem I read made me smile. I did not mean disrespect by that, for it, too, was a grief poem about Lincoln. What I smiled about was a different memory I had. I admit I do not remember much from my high school English classes and especially the parts of them where we discussed literature, but as I read, a clear picture came into my mind. I could clearly recall Mr. Young standing in front of the class and dramatically reciting "O Captain! My Captain!" Some kind of remorse came over me; I think I may have been wishing I had paid more attention back then.

"When I go to work later in the week, I'll remember to share the book with my friend," I thought, and I chuckled again, thinking about the fact that I still did not know his name. I put the book in my saddlebag and headed to town to do some errands. I reached in my pocket for the key and also pulled out a note. "Good reminder," I thought. "Mom taught me to make notes."

That night I drove down to the river to meet a friend. This friend also worked at the store, and he had to close up tonight; I had had the day off. As I drove there and passed the old man's cottage, I slowed. Again I could not see any lights even though I knew about the lights being in the back of the place. I even turned around and came by from the other way but still could not see them. I thought it was amazing that he could be sitting in his old, familiar rocker observing the world go by and I'd never know if he was actually there or not.

My friend and I spent the evening recalling old high school stories and talking about our unique and sometimes crabby boss. And of course we wouldn't be male teens if we didn't talk about girls and say how we sort of wished we weren't sitting on a bench by the river without them. Out of the blue my friend said to me, "You've been kind of weird lately. You must have something on your mind. Anything new going on?"

Immediately I felt defensive and those feelings that maybe my friendship with Jack would be viewed as weird by others welled up in my mind. "No, of course not," I answered. My answer seemed to come out far stronger than I intended and my friend sensed that.

"Well don't get all bothered! I was only asking."

"Ya, Ya, I know. Guess I'm a bit edgy but it is nothing I want to share. Not just yet anyway."

"Have it your way, but don't jump on me about it!"

"Sorry, I didn't mean anything. I'll let you know if you can help or it'll just work out." I fake punched his shoulder as we slid off the table and said good night.

As I left, my thoughts again returned to my new friend. I drove by slowly. As I passed I got to thinking about how such a treasure of experience and warm friendship could stay hidden so easily behind darkness, fear, age, and lilac bushes. I vowed not to let that happen again. I slowed my bike and turned into Jack's drive.

"I see you're out again fighting the mosquitoes," I quipped as I walked up on the porch. It was cloudy tonight with no sunset, so the chairs were set in their usual positions by the window's light.

"They're not bad. They never liked me. I guess I must smell bad or something."

"Yeah, maybe." I fumbled for words, and he motioned for me to sit.

"What are ya carrying?" he asked.

I felt relieved to have him open the conversation, and I sat forward out of the chair that swallowed me up. I handed him the book.

"I had an odd thing happen after I got home the other night. It was late—"

"Oh, yes, you said you were going on a hot date. Good time, eh? I bet it was late!" He smiled at his jab at me.

"Yep," I replied, as I felt warm just remembering those "kisses sweeter than wine."

"Em liked Whitman." He spoke softly as he flipped the pages. "Actually, she liked Whitman better than me!" He chuckled. "His poetry, I mean."

Picking up on his interest, I said, "One poem I found about in the middle of the book struck me because Whitman wrote it about Lincoln after he was killed. I am going to take a history course next term at college that covers that period of history before, during, and just after the Civil War."

"Oh, yes, where was that poem?" he asked as he handed the book back to me.

I fumbled a bit and found it on page 122. "Here it is. It's titled 'When Lilacs Last in the Dooryard Bloom'd.'" I looked up; was that a gasp or a sigh I had just heard?

The man just said, "Why don't you read it, son?"

"Remember, I told you my name is Ron."

"OK, Mr. Ron, read on!"

"There you go again with that poetic stuff." I tried to laugh at my joke, but I could see his look was quiet and he seemed to be deep in thought and feeling.

"Read it please."

So I read: "When lilacs last in the door-yard bloomed, and the great star early drooped in the western sky in the night, I mourned and yet shall mourn with ever-returning spring. O ever-returning spring! Trinity sure to me you bring; Lilac blooming…" I cut off my reading as I began to hear him reciting it along with me.

"Lilac blooming perennial, and dropping star in the west, And thought of her I love."

I looked again at my book where Whitman's line was actually "I thought of *him* I love."

I looked up at his saddened face. His eyes were glistening with tears ready to drop. The drops did not come, and we sat there drinking in the moment for some unmeasured time.

Eventually he said, "Yeah, Em liked Whitman." He breathed in a long deep breath and let out an equally deep sigh.

"I'm sorry," I muttered.

"Oh no, son! Never be sorry to feel deeply, especially about love. My wife's name was Emily—Emily Marie Jackson. She's been gone near five years now, and I feel her sitting here with me all the while still.

"About that poem, you see, Em died in the spring just like ol' Abe. Also, you know those are lilacs out there in the front. She always pushed for us to drive up there every spring. She always said she wanted to do it to check if the cottage made it through the winter, but I knew it was always to see those lilacs out front."

He looked away, and we sat quietly again. A loon called from on the lake, and it was a sort of lonely, melancholy sound that certainly fit the mood. I thought to myself, "I never noticed how neat the loon sounded, especially tonight. I guess I am paying attention more."

"I can't come up here early anymore. Just the thought of those lilacs breaks me up."

"You miss her a lot. I can tell," I said. I was struggling with confusion and feelings I was not used to or sure of.

He looked at me under the worn brim of the old Tiger cap and chuckled. His eyes brightened. "If you're lucky, someday the right lady will be in your life. Maybe that cutie you dated the other night; maybe not. Don't be afraid to love, for though the risks are high, the rewards are higher. The poem and the memories bring tears today, but I wouldn't change a day of my life I spent with her. Emily Marie Jackson." He whispered the name with near reverence.

"Well, now at least I know your name is Jackson. It's about time, for this is the third time we have sat here talking." My comments broke the melancholy, and I was glad to see his grin show again.

"You are so right. Guess I feel like we've known each other for years."

"I'll take that as a compliment."

He reached out his hand toward me, sort of formally. "My name is Jack!"

I eagerly took his hand. It was calloused and rough but tender just the same. It felt good.

"It's good to finally meet you, Mr. Jack!"

"Ha! No, Jackson is the last name!"

"Jack Jackson," I repeated and smiled. "Sort of poetic!" We laughed and smiled. I really felt I was with a friend. My new friend was probably twenty years older than my father. I guess this was a new kind of friendship for me, and I liked it.

I went on to explain all the guessing that had gone on about the name of the cottage. We laughed about the "Jack Shack" moniker. He slapped his knee when I explained how we teens loved to think of it as a haunted place. The *Jack* on the mailbox all rusted and tipped gave a great encouragement to the story that it was haunted.

"That you only come up here once a year in the summer obviously made it seem more abandoned," I explained.

Through his laughter he added, "The old mailbox…It did say 'Jackson' at one time, but I really don't get mail here anymore so I never thought it worth fixin'!" We settled back with our laughter, and he shared more. "However, the sign here on the cottage needs more explaining."

I said, "We could read 'ack,' so we thought it had to be something 'Shack'!"

He laughed and slapped his knee again. "Oh, would Em ever get a kick out of that! She named the place, you know! You see, we had a game we played way back when we were courtin'. When we'd be driving in the night and we'd meet a car with one light out, she'd say, 'One-eyed jack,' and reach over and give me a peck on the cheek."

He reached to retrieve his handkerchief from his back pocket, which was no small task in these deep old rockers. He chuckled as he did it, and I could see those glistening eyes again; I could tell, though, as he wiped his eyes, that his tears now were happy tears. He blew his nose and continued.

"So you see, that became our game. We'd race to who'd see the one-light car first and then laugh. She had a beautiful laugh, and I can hear it still!" The glistening came back, and he dabbed his eyes. "So she wanted to name our cottage 'The One-Eyed Jack,' and of course I agreed."

I laughed.

"What's wrong with that?" he mocked. "We thought it was fun!"

"No, no," I protested. "It's just the discussions some of us kids had about the old sign. We could read the 'the' and the 'ack,' so most thought it was 'The Shack,' like I said earlier, but I always argued there must be more to the name because there was more space there. No, it fits perfectly—'The One-Eyed Jack.'"

We both sighed, recovering from our laughter and settling back in our chairs. Neither of us had noticed it had gotten dark while we were talking. I could see, over Jack's shoulder, a light moving across the water. I assumed it was a boat even though I couldn't hear its motor. The crickets provided their normal loud background music, and as we sat, I heard a car go by.

"You want to hear another good one?" Without waiting for an answer, he went on. "I called you 'One-Eyed Jack' all the time I've seen you going back and forth."

"Me? Why?" But then it dawned on me. "I get it; it must be because of the single light on my motorcycle. Is that it?"

He laughed that infectious laugh again. I was really coming to love it when he did that.

"So you've been keeping track of me going to and from work?" I said.

"Yep. Nothing else for me to do; I sort of keep notice of all that goes on here near the Mighty Clam!"

"We always thought of Dan as the 'mayor' of The Clam, but maybe it should be you. Jack, Mayor of The Clam." I said that and kind of traced it out like a big sign over the road, and we laughed again.

"So that sounds good. Now how old is this Dan anyway?"

"Oh, he must be about your age! Actually, he's probably younger, say, about my dad's age."

"What are you calling me, old?" The smile revealed his humor. "Em would be mad at you for that. She'd always fuss when anyone would quip about being old. She'd say, 'Milk and bread get old and stale and thrown out. I think of us as aging more like good wine or fine cheese.'"

"OK, I'll think of you as sage and aged, not torn, worn, and old!"

"Now look who's the poet!"

"I asked Dan if he knew anyone who had lived or was living here," I said, "and he only recalled an experience thirty or so years ago. He said he was with his father, and they apparently stopped here. You see, Dan grew up in this area all his life. Dan remembered that his dad talked to an older man here. Dan said his father bought a bottle of booze from him."

I noticed Jack's whole demeanor stiffen like there was suddenly a chill in the air. Maybe I had said something wrong or maybe he had other bad feelings about Dan. We sat there for a few minutes saying nothing. I was hoping for some reassurance from Jack but all I got was silence. I knew I had gone somewhere I shouldn't have as he turned and just glared at me.

# 6 - Connections

*It was hard to imagine the old River Clam*

*Being the center of a bootleggin' clan.*

*As a young growing guy without much time behind,*

*History is amazing and surprising to find.*

*Right here under our noses is story of a most glorious kind.*

*Maybe there is more here than meets the eye,*

*More connections reaching, no, not to the sky.*

*Hey, what is that light o'er in the wood?*

*More history ready to be understood.*

His look turned softer, and he sighed again one of his now-signature sighs as he focused and seemed to organize his next thoughts.

"Let me show you something," he said. "Wait here." He went out of sight of the lighted porch.

He was not gone more than a few minutes, and he returned silently with a board that he simply held out to me. I was surprised when I discovered that what he handed me was a piece of rough lumber about sixteen to eighteen inches long and about three to four inches wide. A label or name with letters about two inches high was branded on the piece. The letters were *BFG*, and there was an oval around them. The board was made of relatively thin wood and reminded me of a slat from one of our many apple crates that often had our farm name stenciled on them. As Jack settled back in his chair, I gave him a questioning look but said nothing. He scratched a match, lit his pipe, and let the smoke circle around before he spoke.

"'BFG' stands for 'Benning Freight and Goods.' We are all related somehow to some original Mr. Benning, but I am not sure how. Maybe my daughter can help me sort it out sometime. Did I tell you she's coming up this weekend?"

"No, you didn't," I said as I readjusted in my chair before being swallowed again. Jack relit his pipe. He took a couple puffs and rested his head on the back rest for a while. I was getting used to these pauses in the conversation and wasn't automatically thinking anymore that I needed to fill them with some words.

"Getting ready to close her up," he said wistfully.

I was a bit shaken because I had been enjoying the moment so much and wasn't thinking that summer was ending; I would be going to school in only two weeks, but where would Jack go? I had not even considered this.

"Where do you live the rest of the year—I mean, in the winter? Is it far? Do you live alone?" Suddenly I realized I was stammering out questions and was a bit anxious about Jack leaving.

He put up his hand in his quieting way, puffed on his pipe, and explained.

"I sold the farm in Cass County and moved in with my daughter. She and her family have been real good to me since Em's been gone." He paused, and I sensed those feelings again. "I just couldn't stay out in that house alone. Back to Mr. Benning, my dad married the daughter of Anderson at the store after my mother died of consumption in the early twenties. Anderson was related somehow to Benning. Dad moved here to this cabin, which I always understood was 'in the family' somehow. That was prohibition time, you know. Do you recall what that meant?"

"Yes! No booze allowed!"

"Ha! That is what the laws said, but it did nothing more than start another business called 'bootlegging.' According to what I've heard, my father was the biggest bootlegger in Antrim County!"

"That reminds me. Dan has a picture over in the bar showing Anderson's Store. The unusual thing is there's a group of men outside all lifting mugs or glasses in a kind of toast. What do you think that's all about?"

"I've seen that picture and believe my father may be one of the men, but I've never studied it closely enough to tell. You wonder what they were toasting. The story I was always told was it wasn't so much a toast as a spit in the eye of prohibition."

"What do you mean by that?" This was all new to me, and I was completely enthralled by the adventure of the whole idea.

"Remember I said my father was the biggest bootlegger in the county? Well, that meant there was no shortage of booze in this area. I expect one of those other men in the picture was the county sheriff, who was, as legend had it, the second-biggest bootlegger next to my dad!"

"Whoa! I'm losing the trail here! How does all this fit—first, to this cabin—and second, what does it have to do with this board with 'BFG' on it? I recall the name of Benning from somewhere around here, but I can't recall where."

"Well, you'll have to figure all that out on your own 'cause that's about all I know about Benning. But you asked about the connection between BFG and prohibition. Think about it, son! What would be the easiest way to smuggle booze right in the wide-open daylight and under everyone's nose?"

"You're asking me? I wouldn't make a good bootlegger, but I guess I'd hide it in something."

"Exactly, and what's more natural than shipping boxes that are coming and going all the time on and off boats here at the river? This shipping company had been in the shipping business long before prohibition. They brought lots of goods, from cloth and clothing to boxes of tools and machinery to books and produce— anything you can think of that would be needed in a growing area like here."

"You mean like I might hide fruit from my roommates when I go back to college by putting it among my clothes?"

"Sort of, and think about how these were cases of booze and wrapping them in the center of the shipping box kept them from being detected or hearing them rattle."

"But why here in Podunk River Clam?"

"This is where the steamers came and unloaded cartons that would go by land on to all those little settlements and especially lumber camps up through this North Country."

"Yes, I bet the lumber camps loved to have the booze!"

"No. The cartons were off-loaded here, and my father's crew would open them at night, remove the 'precious cargo,' and seal them back before they would be shipped out the next morning."

"Wow! My mind is wandering off into this fantasy! I can barely grasp all this exciting intrigue going on in this sleepy little place we call home along the Mighty River Clam!"

"Oh, yes, I have something to show you, but it's too dark now. Can you drop by before work tomorrow? I'll help you see how this little bootlegging caper operated."

"You've got me hooked now! I work at eleven in the morning, so I'll drop in around ten if that's OK?"

"Good. Now you skedaddle because I've got some cleaning up to do. My daughter will be here this weekend, and well, bein' alone since Em died..." He hesitated, full of feeling, collected himself, and went on. "Since Em died I'm not a very clean housekeeper. So I need to do some stuff to impress the daughter. See you in the morning." With that and a dismissive wave of his hand, he went inside, and I left with my mind racing.


I didn't go straight home but went over to Dan's Bar. It was a fairly good night customer wise, and no one noticed when I went over to study the picture. I was squinting to try to get a better look in the dimness of the place. I was sort of wondering if I could pick out which man might be Jack's father when someone nudged my shoulder.

"You're studying that picture real hard, son. What do you think you see?"

I looked around to see it wasn't Dan but an older gentleman who I'd seen in here before. I think he was another fishing friend of Dan's and my dad's.

"Yes," I said as I straightened up to speak to him eye to eye. He was a short, sturdy man with a scruffy beard and overalls. He had a nice smile, though the beer breath was a bit strong. I wanted to sound somewhat knowledgeable, so I added, "Yes, this is a picture of this place as it looked in the mid-twenties, I think."

"You're right, young man. Yes, Matt Anderson owned it then, and it was all one place with no wall like that one there separating off the bar from the store. They even had a post office in here for a while."

"Wow! You seem to know a lot. I didn't grow up around here, but I work next door. My family moved to the area about six years ago—no, I guess it's seven now. We live a couple miles north of here on the cheap side of the road, not on the lake"

"That's for sure. None of us can afford that. So what's your interest in the picture anyway?"

I didn't know what I wanted to share or how to share it. "I'm planning to take a couple history classes next year and thought maybe I'd do a paper on our local history."

"Well, must be a college boy, eh? Good for you. I can tell you that picture was taken by my uncle, and they were celebrating—well, I guess I shouldn't say celebrating—let's just say they just got some liquor shipped in and were happy about it."

"But that was during Prohibition!" I said, trying to sound innocent and shocked.

"Well, my uncle worked for some shipping company, and they'd bring these cartons in on the *Mabel* and unload them here."

"The *Mabel*?"

"Oh, yes. See this other picture? That's the *Mabel*, as fine a steamer as ever ran these lakes. It was shallower up past Clam, so they unloaded some of the heavier freight here so's not to drag bottom farther up toward Grass River. They'd smuggled the booze in the crates, so it was simple."

He went on and seemed to enjoy himself and his storytelling, especially when I was an attentive audience. I was, indeed, soaking it all in.

"There's a funny story about the *Mabel* and prohibition. You ever hear the Carling ad that says something about 'Mabel, Black Label'?"

"Oh, yes, I've seen it on TV."

"Well, it seems that the Carling family was brewing beer and making liquor long before prohibition. So they were a bit strapped by the situation and seemed to be in the middle of the so-called shipping company here. So when someone cried 'Mabel' to announce the ship had arrived, it began to be connected to these smuggled booze shipments.

"One of the Carling relatives—I think one of the sons but don't rightly recall—anyway, one of them had a summer home out south of town right about where the Benning Road comes down to the lake. So a whole bunch of locals felt he had stolen the name of our steamer and her deliveries and came up with the new ad campaign. Maybe just a rumor, but it makes a great story, eh?" He laughed.

"Benning Road! I knew I had heard that name somewhere. It's south of here, you said?"

"Yes, just goes up the hill to the east of the lake. It's not a very long road, maybe only a mile. What are you thinking?" He drained the last of his longneck beer.

"Oh, nothing, just more history I guess."

"Well, you come back, son, after you get all that learnin', and look me up. I'll probably still be here." The man looked at the empty bottle in his hand and said, "Anyway, I'm empty." He hollered to Dan, "Hey, Mabel! Black Label!"

Dan scowled at him because he'd heard that joke way too many times. Then he and his pals all laughed anyway as Dan set another longneck on the bar and he returned to his stool.

He never did tell me his name. I supposed my dad could tell me, though, but no big deal. This dead, old place sure was coming alive with memories of the past.

# 7 - Summer Ends

*The end? Can't be! Where from here?*

*My head is full. Not sure what I see.*

*There sure is more to learn.*

*I don't know where to start.*

*Something awaits, and who would know?*

*Is it the history? Is it the old man? Are the feelings*

*All jumbled up in my head? What to show?*

*What to care? Cry the tear? Somewhere there's a healing.*

When I left the bar, it wasn't very late. I didn't have a date, but my mind was still spinning with the ideas I'd just heard about the bootlegger clan here in the ol' River Clam. "That sounds like a bad country song," I thought as I rode my bike slowly down the road. I passed Jack's place and still couldn't see a thing, so I wasn't sure if he was still up or not. I thought for a moment I'd tell him the story I'd just heard in the bar but decided against doing so at this hour.

As I slowly drove, I saw a flash of light off in the woods across the street from Jack's. I let off the gas and coasted; then I saw it again. I pulled over, beginning to wonder if my mind was going wacky with all this intrigue. I sat along the road idling.

I was puzzled and laughed at my mind racing about this strangeness. Was I now seeing lights? Would I hear voices next? Then it came again, whatever it was. First, I thought it had to be fireflies, but I'd never seen them here before—and would there be only one? As I peered into the darkness, there was a dim glow and then a light almost as bright as a flashlight but like one pointed away from me. It disappeared and then appeared again, but this time it moved to the left. It was gone again, and I sat watching for maybe five minutes. Was this another intriguing event to go along with all the rest? I reminded myself to check what might be out in that direction when I came down in the daylight tomorrow. As I restarted my bike, though, I dismissed it and decided it must have been lights from a boat because the river was over in that general direction anyway. I drove slowly home but was not convinced.

I left home early the next day and drove south past the river. I looked at road signs and cabin names. I slowed after a mile or so and pulled along the shoulder at the next gravel road. I didn't see a road sign, so I pulled out and drove on. However, I stopped quickly when I noticed a sign for a cottage pointing down a wide driveway toward the lake. The sign said

"For Brewing and Stewing

Carling and Elkhart Families"

I looked back at the corner from the other side and saw a road sign that read *Benning Road*. I was in luck. It was no wonder I had never noticed it before. It could only be seen from one direction, and I usually traveled from the south here rather than from the north.

I made the U-turn and turned up away from the lake on the dusty gravel. The road climbed steadily up the hill for a quarter mile or so and through a young second growth maple woods. At the top of the hill, I emerged from the woods out into open fields on both sides of the road. They didn't seem to have been plowed in a while, and I guessed they were used these days to grow hay. I couldn't see any farms, but up a little ways, I crested a rise and noticed a lone farmstead up ahead on my right. There were some outbuildings around it but no evidence of much farming action. There were open fields on both sides, and the house looked lonesome. It was your standard rural farmhouse of white clapboard with a large front porch. It sat off the road a ways, but I stopped at the mailbox that read *Erickson, J.* That name didn't fit into anything that I knew of, and I sat there for a few minutes looking at the surrounding area. I could see that Benning Road went gently down ahead of me to a dead end. The north–south road was Cook Road, and I was familiar with where it went. I didn't know what to make of all of this, so I headed back to meet with Jack.

I parked and didn't see Jack at his usual spot on the porch. I called for him. "Jack, are you here?"

"Come to the backyard," he called, and I walked past the porch toward the lake. I couldn't help staring at the lake, which has mesmerized all who have ever lived near it. There were no boats and no loons yet, for it was too early for tourists.

"Hey, give me a hand instead of standing there like a goon." Jack was coming out of the shed dragging something, and I rushed over to help.

"Thanks," he puffed as we lugged several big boards over to the house. We slid them onto the porch and then rested there to catch our breath.

"What are these?" I asked curiously.

"They're shutters for the two big windows. We don't cover the others—just pull the shades. Come back here." He waved for me to follow him again.

We returned to the shed, and he handed me some ropes and some sticks.

"What now?"

"Follow me, and I'll show you."

We walked to the other end of the house, and along the porch I saw some rose bushes. I helped him pound in the stakes around the bushes and wrap them in some burlap he had carried with him. We tied them all up nice and snug.

He straightened after the three bushes were done, held his back, and said, "These are Em's roses that we brought up from the farm years ago. I lost one last winter, and I cried. Em loved roses and pansies." He motioned to the planter on the porch. "Just help me slide this over by the side of the house. I'll have to get more next year, if there is one."

I straightened quickly at his comment. "Don't you think you'll be back next year?"

Jack looked squarely at me, his eyes twinkled, and he smiled a bit. "Each day's a gift, son. I expect I appreciate it a bit more than you, but..." Then he drew near and fingered my chest. "Don't you ever forget it!"

We walked back up on the porch, and Jack sat. He found his pipe. I sat there wondering if I should share what I'd found out yesterday.

"I've got some news," I started. "I found a Benning Road about two miles south of the bridge." I paused, and he puffed. He looked at me curiously.

"By the way, watch the time, for I have something to show you. There'll be no time later."

I didn't understand what he meant about there being no time later but checked my watch anyway. "No problem. I've still got twenty-five minutes before work starts."

"Good." He put down his pipe and slowly pulled himself out of his chair. He seemed to take more effort to do things today, and I wanted to help or offer a hand but hesitated. "Just let an old man get up slowly," he chuckled. "I hope I don't break anything!"

His infectious smile was wonderful, and I followed him again around the end of the porch near the two sheds. This time he went to the one attached to the house, retrieved a key from his pocket, and unlocked the padlock. When he swung the old door open, a cool, musty smell wafted out. He picked up one of those lantern types of flashlights with the big battery on the bottom, like my dad had for night fishing.

"No light down here, so watch your step."

I followed him down some old steps to what I would call a cellar.

"Watch your head. It's good both of us are short—no headroom down here."

I could see some boxes around on a dirt floor in his bright light, and I determined the room had to be about eight feet square. "Pretty standard farc," I thought to myself.

"Here. Look at this box." He shined his light on one of the boxes and turned it with his foot. I saw it immediately.

"There's that 'BFG' stamp or logo again on a smaller box. Couldn't smuggle much booze in that one, could they?"

"No. Maybe that one could have been packed inside a bigger one? That would make it easy to grab out and easier to store."

"What are you suggesting? That this is the place they hid the booze?"

I heard a chuckle, and he moved another step in toward the back wall. He shined his light, and the boards for this wall were obviously crate boards; a number of them were stamped *BFG*. He reached and pulled a string, and part of the wall opened like a door. I was amazed, for the door was not visible but just camouflaged in the vertical slats.

"Here," he said, "is where my dad claimed they hid the booze." He then shined the light, and I could see a framed space maybe four feet wide and the same height as the room; it was about half filled with sand. "I'll bet you want to ask how anything could be stored here. And you are correct that there wouldn't be enough room." He then shined his light high near the ceiling, and I could see farther back into the space.

"You mean it was—"

"My dad told me it was a tunnel and that they hid the booze here."

"Where does the tunnel go?" I asked.

"Well, son, that is a good question. I always assumed it went to the store, for Anderson was certainly the center of the operation. Maybe they brought the booze from the dock by the store and down here. All I know is that it's been caved in with sand like this as long as I can recall. You see, I had never lived here. I didn't move up with my dad when he married Anderson's daughter. I stayed and graduated from Cass High School and got a job. My dad showed me this and told me the story on one of my very few visits—actually, just before he died."

I was intrigued and taking all of this in. I coughed, and he did, too. "Come on. Let's get out of here before we're both sick."

He closed the door with the latchstring hung nearly invisible among the vertical packing slats. We turned back to the steps, careful not to trip. I let Jack go first. At the top I stopped again because the inside of the top door was also covered with packing slats. I pointed to one of the *BFG* logos. Jack just smiled, closed the door, and clicked the lock shut.

I checked my watch. "Oops! I've got to run."

"When will you be out of work today?" Jack called after me.

"I'm out around five," I yelled back over my shoulder as I retrieved my bike.

"Stop over."

"OK."

When I got to work, my boss held the door, handing me my apron and a broom. Without saying anything, I took both and started sweeping off the walk in front. I swept and reconstructed the picture I had just gotten in my brain from Jack's story. I thought of the men in the picture standing in this very place. I paused, leaning on the boom and daydreaming, when the door squeaked.

"I'm all done," I quickly said and hurried in to take over the register as I was scheduled to do that day. The boss just scowled.

The day dragged and five o'clock came slowly.

"In a hurry?" my friend asked and again woke me from my wandering thoughts.

"Yeah, I've got to meet someone."

"Female, I bet! Are you holding out on me?" He mock hit me on the arm.

"No, not so; but do you have plans when you're done closing tonight?"

"No. Why?"

"Remember what I spoke of the other night? I've just got some things I'd like to share, and I think you'll be interested."

"Oh yeah, bait me on why don't you?"

We both laughed. I waved a quick good-bye and rode to Jack's.

I was dumbfounded to find a late-model Chevy station wagon sitting in the drive. It blocked the way, so I parked out by the old mailbox. I walked by the car and saw boxes and a couple of old suitcases in the back.

"Come here," Jack said. "I want you to meet my daughter." The two of them came down the porch steps, each carrying a bag of something.

"This here's Millie. Millie, this is Ron."

I shook her hand; she seemed about my mom's age, which fit the age difference as I had figured it.

"Glad to meet you!" she said and then turned to Jack. "Give me that bag, and you lock the door."

I was visibly shocked, and I know Jack sensed it.

"Well, we're sealed up here," he muttered and turned back, pulling the door closed and turning the key in both locks. Turning back to me, he said, "Well, don't stand there like a dope! Carry this box to the car."

I picked up the small box off the porch and noticed it had in it half a bottle of milk, some bread, and two bottles I couldn't identify.

"What? Are you leaving today?" I knew I was stammering, but I went on. "I didn't think you meant you were going this soon!"

We reached the car and put the box in the backseat. His daughter was already in the driver's seat, and they seemed in a hurry. I struggled with deciding whether to shake Jack's hand, hug him, or both. He broke the stalemate and made the first move. Reaching into his shirt pocket, he pulled out a paper. It was twice-folded, and he took my hand and placed it in my palm. He closed my hand with both of his and looked at me for an instant. His tender eyes glistened again.

"Here, read this and send me a Christmas card. Oh, yes, and study hard, or I might come all the way up here and kick you." He smiled, opened the door, and got in. They both waved and drove away. Now my eyes did the glistening. I stood there by my bike and retrieved my handkerchief, hoping nobody had been watching.

# 8 - What's next?

*First the wonder and the blunder;*

*Next the mystery and the history;*

*Now the newness and the blueness!*

*What's next? I long to know.*

*But his words ring clear about*

*Unexpected gifts throughout the year.*

*In nature we know winter is not only snow*

*But is a time of rest and refresh*

*For in the spring new promises will grow.*


I left with my head in a blur and drove around the corner to the beach area and parked. I went over to the lone picnic table, took a seat, and reached in my pocket. I extracted the paper, opened it, and read the following:

A Poem

Love is a gift.
Don't ever forget it.
Life, love, and time

Are simple and near us, all very fine.
But do we notice?
Some old eyes dim, some young ones slim?
We've shared a gift,
Not expected, not planned.
Life goes like that.
When we're least aware,
We just celebrate; it is a gift so grand.
You remember: work hard,
Don't forget to love along the way.
Know you have touched me
These past special days.

Jack Jackson

August 30, 1963

At the bottom he had written his daughter's address in Cassopolis, Michigan. I didn't even know where that was. My thoughts wandered as I held the paper.

I sat and read it again. I refolded it and put it back in my pocket. I looked out at the lake for some guidance or assurance. I left the beach and walked down to the dock by the river. I sat for a while on the bench at the end and took out the paper and reread the poem again: "Life's a gift, don't ever forget it: Life, love and time, are simple and near us, all very fine." I breathed deeply, trying to take all this in and make some sense of all the things going around in my head. I watched a couple of boats come into the river off the lake. I wasn't paying much attention until one of the folks waved at me. I tried to see the name on the boat because I didn't recognize either the people or the boat.

This reminded me of the mysterious light I had seen the night before. I walked as far as I could along the river, past three or four old boathouses in various states of repair (or disrepair). The last building was a larger one; it was the boathouse for the resort across the street from the store. If I was judging correctly, what I saw would have been behind that building. I could not walk further because the dock ended. I retraced my steps back down the dock and walked on up the road on the other side of the resort past Jack's. I still couldn't believe he had left, and I stopped by the driveway again. I could see those shutters we'd carried were now covering the windows. The cottage again looked as I always thought it had been before: empty and abandoned.

I walked over across the road from Jack's and could barely make out an old, small building in the woods behind the resort. It wasn't on the river, or else I would have been able to have seen it from the river dockage where I had just been standing. It was similar to all of the old, smaller boathouses found at numerous spots on the river.

I stepped off the road into the woods and immediately knew it wasn't a good idea. Mosquitoes notwithstanding, it was very muddy. It was a swamp with numerous rotting mosey stumps and a couple of felled trees. The secondary growth mostly consisted of a tangle of prickly bushes that I could not identify and vines that were everywhere.

I retreated to the road as quickly as I'd entered. As I looked up and down the road and from the second streetlight on my left to the store and bar area on my right, I noticed there was a big dip, with the lowest point being right where I stood. I also noted I was standing nearly in line with Jack's drive, even a little west. I'd never noticed how much this roadbed had been filled in. I pondered all that as I slowly walked back toward the store. It would be closing time soon, and the sun was starting to set over the lake. I stopped at the public beach and sat on the lone picnic table again.

As I looked at the various initials and hearts carved on the table, I again heard the loon. My mind jumped back to Jack and his surprising departure. I felt even lonelier as the sun dropped, and I could see the V-wake of the loon crossing the water exactly through the red reflection of the disappearing red orb. I sighed deeply.

I don't know how long I'd sat there, but the sun had gone and the darkness was increasing. I heard some loud conversation that seemed to be coming from behind me and I turned to see my friend and two companions coming my way.

"I saw your bike, so I knew you weren't gone!" My work partner slid up next to me on the table. "What cha doin' here?"

One of the others who I knew from high school spoke up. "Yeah, what are you doin' out here like a dope. By the way, I saw your bike up at the haunted Jack Shack a couple nights ago. What you doing? Hanging out with ghosts now?" He laughed and poked his friend with the humor of his own joke.

I sensed myself getting tense. "You guys don't have any clue what you're talking about. Besides…" I stopped myself before giving away that I knew the resident of the cabin or that we were getting to know each other.

My friend, Dave must have sensed my sensitivity and spoke. "Oh, give it up you fools. Go back to your game at the bar and I'll join you in a few minutes."

I was relieved when they complied and wandered back toward the bar.

Neither of us spoke for a long moment or two. I was getting good at that but could sense Dave didn't like it. I spoke up first to break the tension. "Thanks for getting those two to leave. I just don't feel like being foolish right now." I squirmed around a bit and Dave lit a cigarette.

After another elongated pause, I said, "I just heard a loon a few minutes ago and watched him slowly cut the wake through the setting sun."

"That sounds heavy! I should write that down and use it in one of the papers I'll need to write for my Creative Prose II class. I'm taking it next semester."

"I can tell sarcasm when I hear it," I said as I pushed him, nearly off the table. "You are about as serious as those two we just got rid of."

"Look out and be careful! I'm not sarcastic. I'm an English major now. You knew that, didn't you?"

"That's a miracle. What do you want to do? Write a book?"

"Not write but I'd like to teach! How about you? Ever consider doing teaching?"

"I guess it sort of runs in our family. You had my mother for a class once in high school, didn't you? I've always admired her for what she did. Did you realize I had my own mother for a class in my senior year?"

"How did that go?"

I chuckled as I remembered those times. "I just never knew what to call her. I just hoped she'd look at me before I needed to ask! I made out OK, but I have no idea how she felt. Guess I should ask sometime, eh?"

The silence returned. We listened as a boat went up the river out to the lake. By the rumble of the motor, we figured it must have been a fairly big one. We heard the motor rev up loudly as the pilot gunned it and raced off down the lake in the opposite direction. The sound quickly disappeared. Dave lit a cigarette, offered me one, and then put them away.

"You never did say why you're still here. You got out of work at five, and that was nearly four hours ago. Have you just been moping around here since then?"

I didn't know how to start, and I took another deep breath.

"Did you ever write poetry in any of those English classes?" I asked.

"Yeah, a few poems, but mostly we studied other writers' poems."

"Like Whitman's?"

"Yes, he is especially good. I remember clearly 'O Captain! My Captain'! It was about Lincoln, and I was taking a history course at about the same time. It all seemed to fit together."

"As Jack would say, 'Em liked Whitman.'"

"What did you say?"

"Here, read this."

I reached in my jean pocket and retrieved the folded paper that was getting a bit tattered by my folding and unfolding. I must have reread the poem three or four times in these last few hours. Dave read the poem to himself and looked back at me quizzically.

"Who's Jack Jackson?"

From where we sat, we could see down the road toward Jack's place, and I pointed. "See that mailbox that's so crooked?"

"Yeah, the one in front of the place that most think is haunted?"

"What does it say on the box?" I said.

Dave squinted in the growing darkness. "I don't know. I can't read that far away."

"Come on then," I said as we slid off the table.

We walked toward Jack's. As we got closer, Dave exclaimed, "It says 'Jack'! You mean the poet lives here?"

"Yep, and he's no ghost, and it is not haunted, and..." I searched for how much I wanted to share. "And Jack and I have become friends."

"But it is empty. If you weren't so dog gone serious now, I'd be bugging you just like the other two. All of us considered this place empty and haunted. Didn't you ever try to scare a girl by threatening to take her in there? That has always been big fun. But now you say you've made friends with the man who lives here named Jack?"

"Yes, it is empty now. Jack just left today, around half past five. He lives with his daughter. You saw the address on the bottom of the paper, didn't you? She or they live in Cassopolis. Do you know where that is?"

"This is crazy in a good way. And yes, one of my roommates my freshman year graduated from there. It's down south of Kalamazoo somewhere, but I don't think I've ever been there."

We strolled back to the bar/store area and continued talking. I shared the short version of my story about meeting Jack in the rain and the numerous talks we'd had since then. I told Dave about how the old man had been sad since his wife's death.

"Her name was Emily, and he called her 'Em.'"

"Thus your statement 'Em liked Whitman' a while ago. You mean his wife liked Whitman's poems?"

"Yes, and Jack wrote poems, too, probably only to her. He only shared one with me, and it was about them watching sunsets together. But when he left this afternoon, he gave me that poem you read, shook my hand, and drove away."

We wandered along and ended up sitting on a bench by the river. We didn't speak then, instead just listened to the sounds of the evening around us. There was a small boat going up the river and some people where noisily enjoying their time in the bar. Dave eventually broke the silence.

"Think you'll ever see him again?"

"Why, yes, sure!" I answered quickly, knowing full well I still had some doubts and fears about it. "He'll be up again next summer." But then I thought about how far off that was, and my feeling of lonesomeness returned. Trying to snap out of this mood, I asked Dave a question on a new topic.

"When do we start closing the store? I've got to be at school two weeks from tomorrow."

"The boss said we pack up on Monday and Tuesday next week and that Wednesday the truck comes to pick it all up. Lots of sales planned for this week with a big ad in the newspaper tomorrow. I too have to get to school soon."

"Have you got any big plans for the school year?"

"Oh, yes, but mostly the same old grind. I'm starting my fourth year and hope to do student teaching in the winter or spring and graduate by June."

"Wow! A college graduate! Who'd have ever thought? Especially some of those high school teachers you used to harass! Me? I'm looking forward to taking a couple history classes. One is on the Civil War, and one is on Michigan pioneer development. Come inside and let me show you a couple of pictures I recently noticed, and I'll tell you what I've learned."

Dave perked up and showed some interest. He tossed his cigarette into the river as we got up from the bench and approached the door.

"Come in! Come in!" he mocked as he held the door. "Enter the historical Clam River Bar! Notice the display of drinkers on the stools to your right!"

I cut him off as we both laughed our way inside. We both knew this was just the beginning of an exciting year ahead and that it would be a long time before we might see much of the Clam again so we'd better enjoy our last two weeks of summer. As the door closed, the loon's call echoed over the water. Maybe it was saying, "You ain't seen nothin' yet!"

ᒧᕽᕼ

# 9 - A Reflection

The River Clam claims a place

And was those years an amazing space

For lots of stuff, for growing and rowing,

For hunting and seeking, for loving and peeking

Ahead, ahead to the further view

Only in the mind visible,

Me without a clue.


When I was a teen,

The river was a mystery.

I was young, full of wonder

About what I would next see.

What if I jumped in

And flowed on and on?

Would I get stuck on a snag?

Or get lost in a pond?

I reflect yet again on the same mystery

And suggest a better metaphor be a tree

That's growing up, higher and billowy.

I seek the sky only to discover

My life's reflected best in the water below me.


The Clam reflects back

Where I was, where I am.

How long and how far

Can I flow with the Clam?


My river flows on, and I find me over rapids

Or other times in a pond on a level plain

Or lost in a big lake or wandering about,

Almost dry and dying, yet I tout and I claim

Those strong current qualities I learned from the Clam!

Grow on! Flow on! Who knows

What the next bend will bring, be it smooth sail or
dam!

# 10 - In-between

*It was Christmas before I returned to the Clam.*

*All was mostly closed up except our friend Dan's,*

*Who kept open on weekends only*

*To give the faithful and loyal their last dose of baloney.*

*Personal changes abound,*

*And I came back and found*

*My curiosity deeper and my wish that my friend Jack was around.*

*But quickly I was reminded of the sagest of thoughts:*

*"Winters are for resting and preparing to grow."*

*So back to college till summer I'll go.*


I didn't get back to the River Clam until just before Christmas at the end of my school term. My friend Dave wasn't home yet, but I drove down to the Clam—I'm really not sure why. The first snow was all around, and the lake rolled with cold whitecaps. I drove slowly past Jack's, and all looked secure. There were no tracks and no loose, hanging boards but just the same old porch waiting for the resident sage to return. "Winter is for resting," That is what he had said. I hoped Jack was getting a good rest in Cassopolis. I still didn't know where it was and promised myself to look it up.

The biggest change from summer was the snowy landscape. I carefully drove on the slippery roads and parked in front of Dan's place. He was only open on Fridays and Saturdays for the locals and the few skiing and hunting tourists. He'd close next weekend, well before Christmas, and stay closed until May.

"Well, Merry Christmas, Captain!" Dan shouted from the other end of the room. The three customers all looked at me; I didn't recognize any of them. But the man in the middle got up and approached me. He was dressed in a hunter-orange overall suit, and I figured out who he was when he stuck out his hand and said, "Well, howdy, college boy!"

"This is right where you said you'd be if I came back." We shared pleasantries, and he hurried back to his brew.

Dan spoke up. "Just home for the holidays, I presume. I'm closing the place up next weekend and having a bit of a party. Why not bring one of those many girlfriends of yours down?" They all laughed at my expense, and I know I began to blush. "Oh, yes," he continued, "see if you can catch your friend Dave. He should be home soon. It will be a good time, and then I'll close it up till spring!"

"That sounds good. I'll try to do both. I'll see you back here Friday." I turned to leave. As I reached the door, Dan hollered.

"And tell that dad of yours to get stocked up on wigglers. I hear perch and gills are biting off Robinson's point and the ice is nearly good enough to walk on up there."

"I'll do just that!" I waved and walked out the door.

It was cold with a bit of snow in the air. I walked over to the river's edge and thought about walking out toward the lake, but it was too windy to go there. So I went to the left—upriver, so to speak—along by the older wharf. The resort had long since been shuttered up for the winter, and there was no life around there now. I eased my way along, for there was some ice on the dock because the wind blew the spray off the water.

I mentioned before that there were some older boathouses and then the dockage for the resort. I stopped at the end and quickly grabbed the post for support. I slipped again and actually sat down; as I did, my hand slid down the post. I was glad for the post and was looking for a safe escape back to my car when my hand brushed over something rough yet curious. I managed to get up on my knees and looked at the back of the post. There was an arrow pointing down toward the water. It appeared to have been carved a long time ago but was still recognizable. The arrow was on the river side of the post so it became even more treacherous as I looked around, actually over the water, at what I thought I had felt. "You've got to be crazy," I warned myself, and I pulled myself closer so I could see over the edge.

I was now lying on the icy dock and getting wetter by the minute, but I was shocked. I rubbed my fingers down the arrow to the oval spot beneath it. I knew *this* would need some explaining: that *BFG* logo, complete with the oval around it, was here. I could not see far enough down, but it appeared to have been carved low on the post, near the waterline.

But why here? If this operation was about smuggling booze, this spot is a good one hundred yards upriver from the bar. I was too cold to figure out any more details. I pulled and, still slipping, managed to get to my feet and slowly head back to my car. As I went I examined all the posts. I counted ten posts, and none of them had any marks or letters on them. I thought about what this could mean as I got in and hurriedly started the car. I sat there for a short while, wondering as I thawed and began to warm. I took off my wet gloves and put them down by the heat vent in hopes that they would dry.

It was getting dark so much earlier now. I turned toward home to prepare for a date—not the same date Jack kidded me about last summer, for we had gone our separate ways. I drove out slowly, checking out Jack's place again. I looked again on the other side and pulled to a stop. Without the leaves on the trees, I could see the old building more clearly. Based on the way it was built up high on posts, I could tell it was originally built to be a boathouse. I thought of trying to walk to it like I had before, but I could see puddles not yet frozen and so I was sure I'd end up in the mud again.

I kept looking at the old building, which was definitely a boat-house, and that made good sense for we were at a river. "But it's not near the river!" I shouted at no one. It made no sense to me, and the *BFG* on the post just made it weirder.

Finally, checking the time—I didn't want to be late—I pulled out into the road. I gunned the car a bit too much, forgetting it was winter. The rear end slipped and swayed on the icy road. I hadn't even driven a car at all since I went to school in the fall and surely not on ice. I had to be careful with my dad's car.

During the fall term, I had decided to change colleges and pursue being a teacher instead of an engineer. I was anxious to share my plans with my friend Dave. My mother (a teacher) was excited not just because I wanted to pursue the same profession as she but also because I was going to her alma mater. It was hard to change plans but exciting just the same.

So I was off to the new school after my Christmas break. In my first term there, I was trying to straighten out transferring credits and decide on my teaching major. That is where the biggest changes came, and I couldn't wait to share what I learned with Jack. My first fun discovery was about the River Clam.

I had planned in my science studies to take several courses, and as I was thinking about a geology degree, I took a course in the Geology Department called Limnology. I don't want to bore anyone with all the details except to explain that limnology is about lakes and rivers and their development. So, for my final project, I chose to do a paper on our Chain of Lakes. The River Clam is about in the middle of this chain. The chain starts up near East Jordan and loops north and then south through Clam and on into two big lakes before flowing into Lake Michigan. The chain is 75 miles long and varies from small mud lakes to deep glacial gouged lakes, with lots of variety in-between to study. I decided I'd share the paper with Jack next summer because I was sure he'd love that kind of stuff.

While I was writing that paper, I found one great resource that was written mostly as an oral history of the area around Clam. It was in that source that I found the answer to two puzzles I spoke of earlier: first, the odd angular placement of Jack's cottage; and second, the strangely placed and seemingly lost boathouse supposedly out in the swamp. It all had to do with an 1875 dredging project, and I had copies of the maps and plans. "Jack would love this stuff!" I thought.

The second course I was planning on taking was about the time before, during, and after the Civil War. As I did research for a final-exam paper, I became interested in investigating the extent of Michigan's involvement with the Union cause. Again, I won't bore anybody with all the details, but the key I discovered was the Clam's connection to one Colonel Mathew Benning. Colonel Benning served in the highly decorated Michigan Brigade and was badly wounded in the Battle of the Wilderness and then discharged. I had yet to sort out how and when he got to the Clam River area, but I knew he became one of the area's earliest settlers.

Jack told me I'd have to do my own research to find out more about the Benning connection, and I believed I had done just that. It explained the road name and the shipping company. I could hardly wait to share all this information.

However, the school year moved along slowly, although I had a lot of new experiences. I kept good notes so I could share it all with Jack, and I thought of him often. I hoped he was having a good winter playing with his grandchildren. I also bet he wrote poetry for them, too.

Spring came around, and I got a call from my boss asking me to return to the store. I got a note from Dave, and even though he was graduating, he wouldn't start teaching until the fall and so we'd be a "store workin' team" once more.

It was nearly June 12 when I got back to the Clam. We were set to start filling and opening the store on the fifteenth. I got the bike out of my dad's storage barn and drove to the River Clam. Just the idea of this gave me a thrill as I thought about "how long I'd been on the lam from the River Clam." I chuckled to myself about that ridiculous line.

Obviously, I was happy about numerous things, including the end of the school year and working again at the store with friends. I was most excited about seeing Jack back at "The Jack Shack" and sharing all the great information I had found.

I pulled up in front of Jack's and was totally surprised and a bit confused because no one was there. He told me last summer that he and his daughter came and opened the cottage on Memorial Day every year. That was his and Em's pattern, and the Memorial Day holiday was the only time his daughter got time off work and could bring him up.

As I sat there idling, a scary thought crossed my mind. What if Jack was sick or something? I struggled not to think of what the 'something' might be but was losing the struggle. I had to go to work. I decided I'd look up that poem and maybe find his daughter's phone number so I could contact them later.

All I could do was whisper a quick prayer that Jack was OK and got up there soon.

☙

# 11 - Returning

*The story started a way back then.*

*Too long ago, so I say, "Back when?"*

*'Twas soon after the State War was done,*

*And it was all begun by a guy named Anderson.*

*The river was different in his day.*

*It traveled to Torch by a different way.*

*But the people were all a hardy clan*

*Who grew and prospered by the River Clam.*

I drove to work one morning later that week. I was still confused and a bit down about not knowing about Jack's condition. Why was he not there? I came around the corner, and my heartbeat soared. There in the drive by the bent mailbox, I could see the rear of Millie's station wagon. I pulled up quickly.

I hurried around the lilac bushes and noticed the shutters were down leaning against the back of the porch. The chairs were on the porch, and I could hear some chatter coming from inside the cottage.

I jumped up on the porch expectantly and just about jumped out of my skin when I heard Jack's voice.

"Good to see ya, son! What took you so long?"

I jerked to a stop. In my rush I hadn't noticed Jack sitting in his old, familiar spot. He smiled and held out his hand. As I happily gripped and shook his hand, I thought he seemed smaller than before, but you know how those chairs were the type that swallowed you up.

"I'm glad to see you, too! What do you mean what took me so long? Where have *you* been? Are you OK? I was worried, but other than 'Cassopolis' you didn't give me any way to contact you."

"Hold it! Hold it!" He lifted up his hand. "One question at a time please!"

At that moment I again noticed the chatter coming from inside the cottage. "That should be enough food. Now don't forget the meat is thawing for tomorrow. Just mix it with the vegetables and pasta in the bowl. You like that, don't you?"

Jack smiled and nodded toward the house. Holding one of his hands cupped near his mouth, he whispered, "My daughter thinks she's my mother!"

"That should do it!" Millie said as she popped out the door. "Oh, I didn't know you had company, and me yapping away!" She seemed a bit embarrassed but no less on task. "I remember you from last fall." She shook my hand. Then, speaking directly to her father, she said, "And remember to feed the cat only half a can a day and make sure it has lots of water."

"Yes, yes," Jack answered, seeming a bit annoyed.

"Oh, yes, remember that Doc John will be stopping every Monday. Don't forget. I put it on the list."

"Don't worry! It's not as if I could or would run off someplace!" Jack quipped.

His daughter sighed impatiently and said, "It's just that I still wish you weren't up here alone. What if—"

"I've got Ron here to keep track of me. Besides, I've been doing this alone for years since your mom passed. Please don't fret."

She sighed again disgustedly and gave up what was obviously an old disagreement between the two of them. She rolled her eyes and checked her watch. "OK, I'm going. I left a reminder list on the table with all the medicine. Dad, I just worry…"

I could sense a teary good-bye was coming, but both were smiling as she leaned down and hugged Jack. "Good to see you again," she said to me. "Wish we had more time to share." And then, quickly enough, she was in the car, and she backed out and drove off.

"Is she driving back to Cassopolis? I did look it up, and it must be about a three-hour drive."

"All of that," Jack commented. "I remember those first years before the highways were improved, it took us most of the day to get here."

I was anxious, excited, and curious all at the same time. I was full of questions. "Does Millie turn on everything for you, like the water and all?"

"No! I have a local guy who lives over on the other lake who comes to turn off the water in the fall and check on the place all winter. In the spring he turns it back on for us. I just call him, and it's all set when I arrive."

"I know whom you speak of. His oldest son graduated from high school with me. He's now in college in Alaska. That sure seems like a long way off!"

"Your school being in the UP is far enough, eh?" He smiled at his traditional UPism of using 'eh' to end a sentence.

"Well, that brings us to my biggest news in a hurry. I have changed schools and am going to school in Lansing now. I decided to change at the end of fall term. So I've been moved downstate since January, which has made me not so far away. It has been a very exciting experience, and I have learned lots of new things!"

"Wow! What are you studying there?"

"Remember I told you my mother was a teacher? Well, I'm going to teach!"

"Teach what?"

"I'm not exactly sure yet. Most likely it will be math or science; those are my two best subjects."

Jack became quiet, leaned back in his chair, and closed his eyes.

"You must be a bit tired by the drive and the moving in; besides, I'm supposed to be at work at two this afternoon. I'll go now and get back to you later. OK?"

Jack smiled and nodded his agreement, and I quietly left. It was so good to see him, but he seemed changed. He seemed older somehow. I decided, though, that I had to quit worrying about what I didn't know anything about.

I had to work a bit late that evening, and it was dark by the time I left the store. I eagerly drove to Jack's. I noticed immediately that all the lights were out. I recalled how tired he had been, and I figured he turned in early. Then I heard a sound I could not immediately identify. I listened more closely. I thought it was a boat motor, but it was lower; I could only describe it as a moan or a low groan. I thought it might simply be Jack snoring, but I listened closely, fearing for him. "Maybe I should knock and check on him?" I thought to myself. Then I heard it again—a low moaning sound that did not seem to come from inside the house as I had first thought. I walked around the left side of the porch toward the lake, and the sound subsided.

As I stood there in the gathering darkness, I was startled when something rubbed my hand. I jumped a little and could see a cat in the faint dusk. He pushed back and forth like a cat does; he certainly was friendly enough. When I reached out and touched him, he began to purr loudly. Could that have been the sound? No, it was something else—a deeper sound—but from where?

Apparently satisfied, the cat walked off and went into the cottage through the loose corner in the door screen. "Handy. In-and-out system," I thought and then smiled at what I'd previously seen only as a sign of Jack's failure to repair the place. I paused again, listening for that sound and hearing nothing, and so then I turned and quietly left for home.

I headed to work early the next day, for I had the long shift. I had to open the store and would not get off until about six or so. I hoped that would be a good time to see Jack and get caught up with each other's winter news.

Dave was at the store when I arrived. "I see your friend Jack must have finally arrived. I saw a car there yesterday."

"Yes, I saw him for only a few minutes last evening. He didn't tell me why he didn't come over Memorial Day as he usually does." I paused, not liking my thoughts and worries, and then added, "He seems weaker and older to me."

"You think maybe he's been sick? How old is he anyway?"

Now that was a curious question, and I was slow to answer.

"Yes, I do wonder about his health, and I have no clue what his age is." I began to share with Dave the few facts I knew. By doing a little math, going back to his mother's death in the twenties and his being out of the home by the time his father was remarried, we concluded he must be in his late seventies by now.

"I guess the simplest thing to do is to just ask!" We both smiled at the obviousness of that answer just as our boss came around the corner and glared at us. We both smiled at her and busied ourselves with the work of the day.

"About time you two did something today," our boss muttered and then stomped off to do whatever it was she did. Both of us had always wondered what that was.

I was pooped when I stopped back at Jack's after work. I dragged myself up to the porch and was glad to see Jack in his chair.

The gathering dark and the light inside gave a glow to his face. He motioned me to the chair. He did not say anything.

I welcomed being swallowed up by the old chair and sighed. "Long day, and my feet are tired!"

"Poor boy!" Jack sarcastically chimed in with his gleaming smile and welcomed chuckle.

"So, smart old man," I said to him, equally sarcastically, "what took you so long to get up here?"

Jack was slow to answer in his patented patient style.

"That reminds me," he said. He pulled himself up out of the chair and moved to the door. It was then that I noticed the new addition. Jack was using a cane to steady himself. As quickly as he went in, though, he was back and handed me a pair of scissors.

"Cut this here thing off," he said. I took the scissors as he rolled up his sleeve, and I saw the plastic hospital band. He pushed his arm toward me, and I cut off the band. He took back both the band and the scissors and placed them on the stand by the window with what looked to be the local newspaper. Then he slumped back into his chair. After resting a short time, he said, "Damn doctors wouldn't let me leave the place. I'm just fine, but they had wires everywhere and dials and tubes. Yuck!" He waved his hands at me in disgust.

I sat quietly. I didn't know much of anything about health issues outside of heart conditions and strokes. Eventually I asked, "What was the problem?"

"Oh, nothing happened. My nosey daughter thought up something and made me see a doctor."

"Yes, and then what?"

"Oh, he was nice enough, but I think the hospitals just want to make money off tests. Poke and prod, take blood, go here, go there. Bah, humbug!"

I smiled, remembering that was a favorite phrase of my grandfather's.

"Well, enough about me. So you changed schools, you were tellin' me. What else did they teach ya, college boy?"

That was the perfect lead-in, and I quickly recovered from my tiredness that was brought on by the day's work.

"Remember I told you I was planning to take a couple history classes? And, by the way, I will get to that later, but when I went to the university, my credits didn't match up real well, so I had to take a science elective. I took a course called Limnology of Michigan."

"Whatever might that be?" Jack quipped.

"Oh, it's very simple actually. It is the study of lakes and streams, of which we have a plenty. I chose to do a study of our Chain of Lakes for my final paper. It was interesting, and I think I discovered something you'll be very intrigued by."

"Me? Why me?"

"You see, I found this great book as I was researching the paper. It was mostly about just this Torch Lake area, including Clam. In it I found a map that I think will explain some things. I've got a notebook in my bike. Wait here. I'll be right back."

As I jumped off the porch, I heard the screen door squeak— though it didn't really sound like it did when it opened fully— but went on with my task. I jogged back quickly and found, there by the door, a cat. It was possibly the oddest cat I'd ever seen. It was kind of a nondescript color and came right up to me like it knew me. Was this the same cat I'd seen the night before? And then I heard that rumbling purr again. One of its ears was smaller than the other, maybe like it had been partially cut off, and it only had one eye. Maybe both conditions were battle scars from a former life?

Jack spoke. "I see you've made friends with the mean part of the family."

I looked at Jack and smiled. I noticed again the conveniently folded-back screen corner and smiled. "No one actually introduced us. But yes, we have met. By the way, whatever happed to it anyway?"

"Oh, I guess some kind of territorial battle at my daughter's. She has several cats, and they fight occasionally. This one showed up one morning all bloody, and my daughter screamed and cried. So what was I to do? I took him to the vet, who sewed him up. I thought he did a pretty good job, all damage considered."

"Well, it's only fitting for you to have a one-eyed cat. Does he have a name?"

I had asked the question and yet immediately caught myself as I saw a big smile come on Jack's face.

"No, don't tell me! Its name must be Jack! One-Eyed Jack!"

Jack and I doubled up with laughter. I couldn't help but believe only Jack would find a wounded, one-eyed cat who could be granted that traditional name, the name of this very cottage.

Jack wiped his eyes with his sleeve. "Oh, wouldn't Em have gotten a kick out of this cat?" He laughed and cried at the same time.

I couldn't help but agree. "I bet she would have loved it! And I bet you would have written a poem about it for her." I could see him getting quieter and more pensive, but I'd learned feelings of love were never bad.

"What about the River Clam? You keep interrupting your story." Jack finally redirected the talk back to where it had started.

I quickly sat forward with my notebook open and drew a picture of Clam and the area around it.

"You see, this is how the river goes now, just straight out to the lake. But it did not always do that!"

"You'll have to show me that. You can't just move a river." Jack was getting more interested and shifted forward in his chair.

"That is what is amazing. Apparently the river originally had a sharp bend to the north about here." I drew more on my paper, showing the channel turn. "I guess the lumber people had pushed for this change because it was difficult to get logs out past that bend where they were inclined to pile up and get stuck. Also, it was dangerous for boats coming in from the south to go north and make this big turn back into the river channel. I guess it was especially dangerous when there were high waves and they could easily get thrown up against the rock jetty placed about here out into Torch." I drew some more. "It seems the Corps of Engineers did a whole lot of channel work in different sites around the whole chain in about 1875. It showed the maps in that book I referred to earlier. Specifically here at Clam, they simply cut the channel straight through as we have it today. It was a relatively short distance, and mostly the area was a grown-over sand dune besides, which made for easy digging. Our professor described seeing that feature on other streams coming into any big lake. The predominantly west–southwest winds push sand up onto the shore, and the mouth of the river is pushed northward."

"Yeah, you know there is only sand on this, the east side of the lake. There are no natural beaches on the other side." Jack spoke interestedly, and that made me feel important, like I had really learned something.

"Now this is the exciting part!" I said and drew in Jack's cottage and how it was at a strange angle.

Jack immediately saw what I was implying. "Well, damn!" he said. "The ol' Clam once flowed through my front yard!" He sighed and looked out, using his imagination. He finally shook his head, smiled, and settled back.

"Well, son, you did learn something at the big ol' school, didn't ya?"

I smiled. "There is another thing in this mystery these facts might explain."

"What's that?" Jack asked.

"It is that old boathouse across the road that's back off the present river. Maybe it was on the original river?"

Jack's eyes narrowed and he seemed to look out through his eyebrows. I had seen that look before, but I wasn't sure if it was a good or a bad sign.

"I've always wondered about that place," Jack said as he stroked his chin, appearing thoughtful. "Others have told about some strange things that have happened around there."

Remembering the light incident I had seen, I asked cautiously, "Like what?"

Before Jack could answer, I heard that sound again. I looked at Jack and could tell he'd heard it, too. It came a second time, a long, low moan or groan. Well, I was sure now that what I'd heard wasn't Jack's snoring or the cat's purring.

Jack spoke first. "Once I thought that sound came from that old shack out there in the swamp. You'll really think I'm crazy pretty soon if I tell you more. But, you know, sometimes I am sure the sound comes from that old tunnel I showed you behind that hidden door."

We looked at each other. We didn't say anything and just listened. We both jumped when the screen door suddenly creaked. One-Eyed Jack was there, and he looked to be wondering what all the fuss was about.

# 12 - Colonel Benning

*How could a war so far away and so dammed*

*Reach all the way north to our River Clam?*

*Many a man stepped forth to defend*

*The Union that had provided so much*

*For them to live and grow and mend.*

*Immigrants from far away and rough lumbermen*

*From the woods did they call forth and fight*

*To love their Union another day.*

*Conflict touches all in different ways.*

*Some died, some wounded and*

*Carrying their hurt and pain every day.*

*One man's debt to an unknown we found.*

*He came to the Clam, to repay the debt*

*He was to go underground.*

The store was opened and running, so *busy* became our middle names. Summer was in full swing, and those who didn't have to work had watched the fireworks on the Fourth. It was getting hotter. I stopped to see Jack later that week. He got right to the point with his first question, picking us up right where we had left off.

"Well, tell me what you learned about Benning," he said. Then he got more hospitable and offered me a glass of iced tea that he had sitting there waiting. I was hot and willingly accepted, drank some, and relaxed.

"Where should I begin? First, our Mr. Benning was actually one Colonel Mathew Benning, US Cavalry attached to the Michigan Seventh Cavalry, which in turn was part of the Michigan Brigade. Some called them the 'Fighting Fifth' because part of the brigade was from the Michigan Fifth Cavalry. They are also referred to as Custer's Rangers and go by several other titles. One thing is obvious, and that is that Michigan sent many units into the war, and many fought some of the worst battles. Also, Michigan units were often responsible for turning defeat into victory. Here is the beginning of the paper I wrote." I handed Jack the introduction I had written, and he read it aloud.

"Michigan's involvement in the Civil War is well documented. From the earliest call after the April 1861 firing on Ft. Sumter, South Carolina, Michigan responded mightily. Many have asked why so many Michigan folk who were mainly homesteading pioneers would walk off their land to fight a faraway war. I have read numerous explanations and will try to summarize the various reasons here.

"First, many were immigrants and felt extreme obligation to the country that had given them a new home and new opportunity. In my own family, I had a relative participate in the war, and he had only been in this country for about five years having immigrated from Canada. Secondly, many were simply rough and tough lumberman types who wanted to go out and whip those 'Rebs' to teach them a lesson. They were probably not very knowledgeable of politics or government but simply sought a good fight and were convinced this was an important fight to join. Thirdly, most Michigan folk responded out of extreme patriotism and their desire to keep the Union together. I mention this to make the point that Michigan units were seldom concerned with the matter of slavery. Generally, most in Michigan had no close contact with slavery and had no feelings about it one way or another. The abolitionist movement was present here in the state, and the Underground Railroad was operating, but it was not general knowledge and did not enter into their reasons to fight."

Jack looked up from his reading, stroked his chin, and reached for his pipe. We sat in our normal quietness as he fussed with his pipe and tried to light it a couple of times. There was a breeze tonight, and he cursed the matches that got blown out. Then he responded.

"This is good stuff, son. Thank you for sharing, but you haven't said much about Benning. Did you say he was a colonel?"

"I'll get to more of that. I wanted to explain this was an entry-level history course, so we didn't get real deep into any topic. Thus, for this paper and for my measly three credits, I was not expected to complete a Sandburg or Catton look-alike volume. The professor seemed to want us to get a feeling for the war. He stressed learning about some soldiers' and the government's feelings and in turn developing some feelings for the war, not just learning a lot of facts. The university has many civil war records. The professor had put a representative collection on hold at the library. The list included some of the large writings, like Sandburg's, but others were more personal. One book was full of newspaper articles from a smaller eastern newspaper. It seemed to concentrate on local units and people who were involved in different battles. My professor felt the most valuable and most arduous to pursue were personnel writings. Therefore, he had reserved several personnel diaries and excerpts of diaries. One on reserve was literally the blown-apart pages of someone's writings. That was a graphic reminder of the war for sure. One diary I spent some time reading was written by an Irish soldier from near Grand Rapids who had joined the Muskegon Rangers early on and returned after the war to live in Muskegon. I wish I could have interviewed him personally, but I'm sure he's long since passed."

Jack was paying close attention, and that urged me to continue. I wanted the paper to speak for itself so I read on:

"I read with deep interest the feelings of one unnamed Union officer who shared his thoughts about two particular days of some battle. He wrote:

I am weary of this conflict and I find such needless loss all around. Two of my company's men had the duty of clearing the dead and wounded from the battlefield tonight. I cannot write anymore now for the description is simply too revolting even for me, an officer.

The next day this officer wrote:

One of my Company commanders brought to me a young Confederate lieutenant who had been captured. He looked so young, and I cannot imagine him to be over twenty years of age. He acted angry and sullen, which I had no trouble understanding. Trying to make him comfortable, I asked if he would talk to me if I removed the cuffs and chains. His dark eyes scowled at me but softened slightly as he agreed. I did as I had promised and asked my aide to leave us alone. The young officer stood at attention, and I nearly had to force him to sit in a chair. I asked him some questions, and he would only answer a brisk 'yes, sir' or 'no, sir' until I asked if he had family and where he was from. I could see the man's anger and bravado melt, and I pictured this could be anyone's young son sitting before me. He shared about a young wife and parents on a farm in Tennessee. 'In the mountains,' he said with an almost reverent remembrance. Sensing tears and emotions, I quickly changed the subject. After the young man left, I couldn't help but confirm again the ridiculousness of this war. He and I had changed from enemies to men. Oh God, save us all and get us home."


I paused again in my sharing and began to feel the same emotion I remembered I felt when I was first reading the material. I looked at Jack, and I could tell he, too, was feeling deeply the passion and pain shown in these writings. There was simply nothing either of us could do to expand on these details, so we just sat with our feelings.

I broke the silence.

"Someone else had done some research on Michigan Union officers, and it was in that document that I found a short reference to Colonel Benning. Let me find it." I leafed through my notes and handed Jack a page from my paper. He took it, adjusted himself in the chair, and sipped his iced tea as he read out loud:

"I found in the university collection an interesting entry about one Colonel Matthew Benning. It appears that Colonel

Benning was lost in a battle and his partial diary was found in the saddlebag of his fallen horse. Colonel Benning was not found and presumed dead. The diary was found at the Battle of the Wilderness in Spotsylvania that occurred on May 6–7 of 1864. The battle itself was between a large Union Army outnumbering their Confederate foes two to one. The crafty General Lee knew the bad odds and drew the Union Army into battle in the thick woods. The battle was fierce and very difficult to fight in any traditional way. Artillery was nearly useless, and most fighting was at very close range. To add insult to all that, the only thing the artillery really did was set the forest on fire. So with fire and heavy smoke everywhere, the close-order fighting became even more difficult, and there were many losses.

"Colonel Benning's body was never found as the battlefield was cleared. He was presumed killed in battle. Because of the fires, many bodies for both sides were never able to be identified. The remains that were found were hastily collected in mass graves and buried.

"Curiously, in November of 1864 (five months later), Colonel Benning walked into a Union Army post in western Virginia. He had obviously been badly wounded, and his arm had not healed well; he kept it in a sling. Most obvious was that he had been burned from the fires that occurred during and after the battle. He explained he had been thrown when his mount had panicked in the fire. He must have been knocked unconscious. His wounds had healed, but he was, according to the army report, badly scarred, especially on his face. He was given a military discharge and sent home."

Jack set back seeming to think deeply about what he had read. Then he spoke, "This is a lot to take in at one sitting. Will you leave your paper with me to read more slowly?"

"Oh, yes. I'm so glad you find it interesting."

"Let me get this straight," Jack said with a questioning look on his face. "You're saying our Colonel Benning was not really killed in the Battle of the Wilderness but was somehow saved? But he was gone for what? Five months? Do you think he may have deserted?"

"Absolutely not, and even the army did not expect that. Apparently, the extent of his injuries and his story were enough to convince them. They agreed and immediately sent him home discharged."

"But who do you think saved him?"

"I have no answer to that question. I would love to uncover some more information someday. Maybe I'll take more history classes just for that search alone. As I read the limited parts of that diary, I gathered that he seemed to have no animosity toward anyone, including the Confederates. He certainly had no warmth for the slave issue and spoke candidly about the Negro unit fighting along with them. He doubted their skills but had no time to elaborate before he was killed—I mean wounded and then saved by some kind group or family who certainly cared for him somehow."

"They must have been *real* kind!" Jack said. "Didn't that one account say he had a badly injured arm and extensive burns? Some caring Southern family must have looked after him." After a thoughtful pause, Jack added, "Or a family of…You know, it could have been a colored family."

"What? I doubt it!" I said with more shock in my voice than I expected.

Jack said, "Think about it for a moment. Which is more likely: a southern *white* sympathizing family or a southern *negro* sympathizing family?"

"But…" Then my mind began to collect a new vision of the historical happenings. I also needed to sort out how this new understanding was to affect me today.

"Speaking of that…"

"Speaking of what?"

"Well, we weren't speaking of it, but my life at the university has been a real eye-opener. For one thing, I have never been around so many young Negro people. I certainly never knew any Negroes around here! Not in good old white Clam River!"

"Son, you are growing up in a different time than I. When I grew up in the Cass area, there were numerous Negro families. Some went to our school. Some were farmers, and worked together with all of us on the local farmer concerns and organizations. I never was bothered about it. Mostly, back then, people just kept to themselves, and no one really cared."

"I never knew there was such a mixed population in that area of Michigan."

"I have a book you can borrow that will shed some light on that area. Remind me before you leave and I'll get it for you."

"Thanks. That'll be great. At school I have a new friend who's in our church youth group, and his name is Lenny. He grew up in Flint. He's from an average family; I think one of his parents is a teacher, like in my family. He said his high school was nearly half Negroes and half whites. He has had such a different view of things, and I'm learning a lot from him."

"Say, are you beatin' around the bush at somethin'?"

I was caught a bit short by Jack's frank question and had to admit that I guessed I was. I reached in my notebook, pulled out the letter, and handed it to Jack. He read it over quickly. There was another thing that fascinated me about Jack: he didn't wear glasses and seemed to have perfect sight, near and far. All the older people and even a lot of the younger people I knew wore glasses; even I had begun to wear glasses since last year.

"I've never seen a— what is it called, a minstrel show? Why does it concern you? What is it anyway?"

I thought for a minute to try to explain, and then said, "It is a kind of comedy show with singing. There are a lot of funny, silly joke skits; some are just plain dumb, sort of slap stick stuff, you might say. The local men's club has done it for several years. My dad is a member and knowing I liked to sing got me involved the last couple years."

"That sounds like fun! What seems to be your concern?"

"My concern," sounding rather indignant, "is that we were just talking about the possibility of it being a Negro family that helped Colonel Benning. A minstrel show is all white people in black face makeup. That seems like we're just making fun of Negroes. Many of the skits, jokes and much of the language is all exaggerated negro stereotypes."

"Like what?"

"Oh, you know, like Jack Benny does with his butler Rochester. They imply Negroes are all lazy and only eat watermelon besides talking funny; stereotypes like that. They speak in slang like saying, *Yous knows Mista Jones*. Oh I don't think I'm making any sense." I stopped and held my head in my hands.

"I can see you are upset but excuse me asking, but why is it a problem *now*?" Jack leaned toward me trying hard to understand my concern.

I was slow to answer, but I had grown comfortable with the silence Jack and I shared; here it helped give me time to gather my thoughts.

"Now? Now it feels different. I don't want to wear blackface and what? Play like I'm a Negro? I feel like...like I'm making fun of those people and, specifically, my new friend Lenny."

We both got quiet again. Jack rustled around and found his pipe. He fussed with it and pulled out a match, but before he lit the pipe, he looked at me and spoke.

"The doc and my daughter think I should throw this thing away. In fact, I thought she had done just that." Then that twinkle showed in his eye as he scratched the match and lit up, leaned back, and enjoyed several deep, aromatic puffs. I had to admit I didn't mind his smoke at all.

Another characteristic of Jack's was that he never tried to solve any problems or concerns I voiced. He only listened and made a few comments. So I was not expecting him to solve this dilemma swirling in my head. He handed my letter back to me.

"You'll work it out. I know you will; you're a good thinker, boy. Oh, yes, that reminds me of something." Jack got up slowly. I got up to help him, but he waved me off and threatened me with his cane. We both laughed. He went inside and returned shortly with a book. Jack the cat appeared again, taking advantage of the open door instead of going through his scratchy hole in the screen. Jack handed me the book as he returned to his seat. He was a bit tired and took a couple minutes to catch his breath. I flipped through the pages as he rested. Then his voice grabbed my attention away from the book's contents.

"Millie got that for me for Christmas. I had always known there were connections in Cass County, so I was interested. Just last year they started a movement or fundraiser or whatever to build a permanent monument to the Underground Railroad and that one lady. What's her name? Well, you'll find out for yourself as you read, and we'll discuss it. By the way, my daughter is coming up for a couple of days, so keep it, and we can discuss it later."

As he returned to his pipe, I felt a great deal of peace; I didn't feel that I'd found any solutions, but I was experiencing peace of mind. That was good enough for now. We listened as the sound of the loon echoed across the breeze. It was too dark to see any wake on the water, but just knowing the loon was there had a calming effect on me. Just knowing Jack was there had a calming effect also.

# 13 - Changing View

*Sometimes I wonder what I'm going to do*

*When the world opens up to give a different view.*

*One generation learns from the last,*

*But the new group can't just accept the past.*

*That's how the world turns, even here in the Clam.*

*My mind is confused as I struggle and learn*

*And cram in new outlooks I've found on the lam.*

*"No, I don't want just to be taught.*

*I want to make up my own mind," and I know I can,*

*For I come from the hardy stock of the River Clam.*

"What are you writing?" my dad asked.

"Oh, just some notes."

He paused and went on piddling with his yard stuff. I remained seated at the picnic table in my folk's backyard, sort of lost in thought.

"I don't think I've ever seen you think so hard. That move to the university upset you somehow?"

"Oh, no! That has been an exciting decision in many ways. I'm so glad I made the change. It took some getting used to. I love it!"

"However, do I hear a 'but' coming?" He spoke as he sat down with his ever-present coffee cup and thermos. "Learned to drink coffee yet? Want a cup?" He asked and filled his own.

"No, and no, thanks!" We both chuckled. "I guess I can't have many of the family genes if I don't drink coffee." My dad smiled and raised his cup like a toast before settling back in his lawn chair.

"So, what's got you so unsettled anyway?"

I reached under my pad of paper, pulled out the letter, and handed it to him.

"So you got the letter, eh? I told Jim, this year's chairman of the show, to ask you himself. I know you've sung in it before, but I wasn't going to commit for you. Did you just get it?"

"No, I got it during finals week just before I left school. I just tucked it away, but I got a reminder at the store yesterday when... Did you say his name was Jim? Anyway, he said he knew you and knew who I was but had just happened into the store. He asked if I could help with the show."

"What's he want you to do?"

"Just sing in the chorus and do a short routine of 'I've Got Rhythm' with two other guys. He thought that was all but really couldn't be sure."

"Sounds simple enough," my dad said in response.

"Yeah, but rehearsals start tomorrow night!"

"So?"

"I guess I don't know how to approach this. You see, my being at the university has opened my eyes to a lot of things, things I had never thought of before."

"Like many beautiful girls, I would guess!"

I rolled my eyes as I always did at my father's comments about my girlfriends.

"No, not that." I paused again and then asked, "Have you ever had a Negro friend?"

Silence and a deep look came from my father. He sipped his coffee and looked over the cup that he held in both hands.

"Son, when I was in the army in forty-five and six, there were white units and separate black units. When we were in Hawaii, a black unit was housed right next to us. Many of the guys in our outfit were very upset. Me? I don't know. As long as folk are decent, they don't bother me."

I smiled.

"What? Did I say something wrong?"

"No, it's just that I was thinking before you walked up here about all the different people I'd met and worked with because of the farm. You sure could collect a variety of folk! I think of the deaf guy, Jerry, and the toothless hired man. Remember Mom never liked him?"

He acknowledged what I said with a nod, and we both laughed.

"Yes, and I think he's the one who stole all those antique tools."

"It was an unusual bunch. I also thought about some of the cherry pickers, like Pete and the Dewey family. Very interesting people, not in a bad way—I don't mean to criticize at all—but I think it helps me to enjoy the people I meet now and try to get to know them better."

"And we can't forget some of the customers who came to the farm!" He put down his cup. "Do you remember Mrs. Camp?"

"Oh, yes!" We laughed again, for this was indeed his favorite story. "She never liked me," I said through the laughter. "Mom always teased you about how Mrs. Camp loved to buy peaches and apples but only from you!"

"Yes, but you were always there, especially when that cute granddaughter of hers was there. Right?"

I rolled my eyes at him again.

He got quiet for a moment. "Getting back to your original question, do you remember the Negro family who came up for apples every year?"

"No, but maybe they came later in the fall after I was in school. I don't recall ever seeing or meeting them."

"They came from over by Mancelona. They called him 'Nigger Joe.'"

I cringed, let out a "yuck," and scowled.

He looked at me oddly and said, "That bothers you?"

"That's it in a nutshell, Dad. At the university lots of different folk are around me all the time. I found myself uncomfortable at first, but like you said a while ago, 'If they act decent, they don't bother me,' and I agree. One young man in particular is in our church group. Lenny is a quiet guy and very smart. We've talked a lot, especially about our different backgrounds. He's from the city, and I'm from a small town. His high school had several thousand kids and mine a hundred. You know what the similarity was that has brought us closest? Both of our mothers are teachers! So we've become fair friends."

"Speaking of decent, did I ever tell you or do you maybe remember the snowstorm back in 1958?"

"No, I don't remember anything special about it. Why?"

"Well, it seems that Nigger…I mean, Mr. Joe and his family live along the highway north of town, and the storm stranded many folk. N...Joe went out and brought some of them out of their stranded cars and into their home. I understand it wasn't much more than a two-room shack. But all were warm, albeit crowded, and waited out the storm. Next day, plows came and opened the road, and after lots of shoveling and pushing, all were out of the snowbanks and on their way."

"Wow, they sound like a nice family."

"Well, yes, I guess they were. But the best news was that one of the stranded people was a truck driver for some grocery chain. Several weeks after the storm, he pulled back into their drive, and his boss came with him. They gave Joe and his wife a big 'thank you' plaque. Then they opened the truck and delivered all-new appliances: a stove, a refrigerator, and a washing machine. Plus they left lots of groceries."

"That's pretty neat!" I responded.

Then my dad got quiet and scratched his unshaven chin.

"You know, I heard that story from the grocery people over there. You remember the Lebanese family who ran the store where your mother always liked to shop? He told me the paper wouldn't even print the story. His grocery company was looking for some good publicity, but they wouldn't print it."

Rubbing his chin and pouring himself more coffee, he seemed lost in thought.

Talking with Jack, I'd gotten better at silence, so we just sat. I picked up my papers and began to make some more notes. Dad spoke up.

"So you never have told me what you were so concerned about."

I took a breath, collecting my confused thoughts. I took another breath and let out a long sigh.

"Don't you think it's a bit of a problem doing a minstrel show? I mean blackface and all? Why do we do such a show anyway?"

My dad shrugged and replied, "Well, I don't know but minstrel type shows have been around a long time. I don't remember when I first saw a show done in black face but I am sure it was around long before my time. I remember one example. The Bing Crosby movie White Christmas that your mother likes so much came from another movie called Holiday Inn. Have you ever seen that one?"

"I am pretty sure I haven't."

"Holiday Inn is about a guy who gets tired of show business and opens an inn where they only entertain on holidays. That is where the song White Christmas was first presented for the holiday of Christmas. In the Holiday Inn movie they had another holiday and did the songs all in black face. I don't recall why but they did."

"So, didn't it seem odd?"

"Well, no. Actually it was just funny."

I jumped to my feet and interrupted him, "Making fun of others and carrying on those dumb stereotypes was funny? It doesn't seem right to me!"

"Son, calm down and listen. I think you're growing up in a new world. It will be a lot different than mine. I'm glad you're more open-minded than many of the folk around here. Don't tell our pal Dan about this, for I know he'll go off for sure!"

Dad had to leave for work. I had to go soon, too, but I sat for a while. I still didn't know what to do. I was glad Jack had shared earlier and was glad my dad had listened and shared, too. As I sat I noticed the encyclopedia set on the shelf. That gave me an idea and I pulled out the index volume. I looked up 'minstrel show' and was directed to volume 'B'. I opened it to "Broadway Shows", leafed a few pages and found the section on 'minstrels'.

I read for a while and learned the minstrel show had been around since before the Civil War. I was surprised. I found it defined as: *a variety entertainment show usually done in blackface using black cultural images, jokes and exaggeration.* It said it was even done sometimes by black entertainers. Interest seemed to be based on a deep fascination white audiences have about the Negro culture, especially the music.

"Interesting" I thought, "seems to be innocent enough." However, I could not get rid of the unsettled feeling in my gut. I put the reference book back in its place on the shelf.

I pulled out Jack's book and read the title. *Underground Railroad*. I sat some more and read.

Later I went to the rehearsal. I was full of mixed feelings. I recalled how all my years growing up "nigger" was such an easy word for my dad to say but never for me. Near the end of high school, I participated in a regional track meet—I can't recall which. I clearly remember there was a team there from Covert that was mostly

Negroes, and I remember being in the locker room with them. I had heard prejudiced, exaggerated stories for years, and yet these guys seemed just like all the rest of us. But I knew I was uncomfortable then, and some of that same confusion and discomfort was hanging on me now.

The rehearsals didn't make it any better. In fact, they only made me feel more confused. We were practicing the same old prejudiced lines, exaggerated speech, and actions of Negroes but with a new twist. At the second rehearsal, in came four Negro men who were to be the musicians for the show. It seems they were playing that summer at one of the big resorts. It was the one that was trying to be a "year-round resort" and not just a ski area. They had a gorgeous restaurant there, and this group was employed for the entertainment.

This just compounded my confusion. How could these white men act out such foolish stereotypes and in front of some Negro men besides? I wondered how those men felt. I was shy to talk to the musicians but when I did I discovered they were kind gentle guys just making a living doing their music. They even made some stereotype jokes about white folk trying to act like Negroes. I guess shy is another word for fear. Fear and ignorance seem to be the key to most of this being uncomfortable around people different than I am used to. When thinking of how I had changed in the past year it was simply having new experiences to overcome that ignorance.

I never did resolve anything that summer about minstrel shows, but the experiences I gained helped me begin to understand people who were different. The feelings I was having were very similar to what I was thinking last summer about what I'd learned from my friendship with Jack. This time I was learning about people of different color, whereas Jack was someone of a much different age. Differences come in all sizes, shapes, ages and colors.

Just thinking that out helped me. Later I remembered what my dad had told me about the family in Mancelona who had helped others in the storm. I decided to seek out more information for myself. I guess, even with all this resolve, I was still scared to go alone, but I didn't think anyone else in my little town would care like I did. "Hold it," I thought. "That's a kind of unwarranted prejudice in and of itself."

But anyway, I decided to try to learn more and affirmed right then "I was headed for Mancelona" without a clue of what I was doing.

౬౨

# 14 - Librarian

*Who'd have thought? Who'd have known?*

*I am as befuddled as can be!*

*Right here, ten miles away, is a new family,*

*But I would never have crossed*

*Over society's rules and barriers,*

*If not for this curiosity, I would have lost.*

*Youth has great advantage,*

*For not enough fears have built in*

*To keep from searching and asking*

*And such, so here I go wandering to the unknown again.*

I drove north of Mancelona up the four-lane part of the highway. I passed through the next small burg and went on to the endless flatness of the potato farms. When I first discovered this area, I was astonished at the flatness. We lived to the west, nearer Lake Michigan, where the glacier tongue digging out the big lake had left large deposits in its retreat. We happened to live and farm the top of one of those features known as moraines. Nevertheless, our side was full of hills, whereas twenty miles away was this potato-rich flatland I was traveling through today.

It suddenly dawned on me that I had no clue what I was looking for. All I'd been thinking about was my dad's recollection that the family lived along the four-lane part of the highway north of town. I didn't even have their names, except for the derogatory one my father shared.

As I thought, I slowed to a stop along the road. I suddenly had a new idea, took what was possibly an illegal U-turn, and returned to Mancelona. It is a small town, and it only took one swing around the village to locate the library.

I walked in confidently. But when the friendly lady at the desk asked, "How may I help you?" I was suddenly at a loss for words. How could I explain I was trying to find people whose names I didn't even know? She was patient and asked again pleasantly, "Are you looking for something specific?"

I finally sorted my thoughts and told her about my search. I had heard of the "storm story," I said, and I hoped to find and interview the family. Was she aware of the story and/or the family? The questions began to tumble.

She was kind again. "Are you a reporter or performing research for a paper maybe?" She smiled, looking over her half-glasses, but seemed mildly cautious, maybe even protective.

"It's a bit hard to explain, ma'am," I answered. "I'm on a bit of a personal quest; however, even that makes it sound way too noble. But, yes, I am researching some connections I have discovered between a Civil War veteran and my area of Clam River."

"Oh, you're a Clam River rat?" She laughed a quiet giggle. "That is what my brother called some of his friends from that area! I didn't mean to offend you." Her expression turned to one of concern.

"No, no offense taken," I responded and smiled. "We wear that name proudly, if you can imagine that."

After we had cleared the air, she cut directly to the task at hand and brought me back to the reason for my visit.

"Perhaps you can tell me specifically a name you are trying to find. We have some fine records here collected by a former librarian whose family was also connected to the Civil War. Maybe there will be something in those materials?"

"That may be very helpful, but first I'd like to find a family, a Negro family that lives near here."

She caught my eyes again over her glasses, squinted slightly, and then replied, "Mr....ah, you didn't tell me your name, young man."

"I'm sorry, ma'am. That was rude. My name is Ron, and I see by your nameplate that you are Mrs. Robinson. I do so appreciate your help."

"Well." She paused, seeming to be thinking over something. "You seem like a sincere young man."

"Oh, no, ma'am, my father shared a story about the negro family helping people being caught in a blizzard some years ago."

"Yes, it was in the winter of 1958—around February, I believe, but we could check that accurately by looking at the back copies of the paper that are stored here in the back room. I believe the story your father shared included people being brought in from the storm by Jonas and his wife—"

"Then you do know what I am talking about? The story and the people are real?" I was excited and grinned from ear to ear.

She held up her finger to her lips like a librarian would to shush someone.

"Yes, son, err...Ron, was it? Jonas and his wife are the people you speak of. However, not everyone around here is always nice to them. It's a shame; they are such gentle, helpful people. But let's get back to your research. Excuse me for sounding cautious, but I've heard some sad stories."

"Like what?"

"Oh, kid stuff mostly, such as dead animals thrown in their yard or drive-by name-calling, that sort of thing. I guess my husband and I have always tried to be good neighbors and sort of look out for them. My husband is a builder, and he often has Jonas work for him. He is a talented carpenter, my husband says."

"Can you give me directions to their home?"

She became quiet, looked away, and fussed with some papers on her desk. Then she said, "Come with me and let's see if we can find the newspaper article."

I followed her to a room full of shelves covered with what looked to be mostly old dusty books and junk. She stopped at one set of shelves and handed me a large stack of newspapers. "Please take

these over to that table. That stack is labeled 'Mancelona Paper –
1957-1960'. We should find the article here."

I did as directed and pulled out two chairs.

"No, this is your job. I must get out to the front desk. Just be
gentle with the papers and be sure to keep them in order. You can
work here as long as you want and will not be disturbed. Good
luck!" She turned and left me in the musty store room.

I felt a bit upset. I had come here to meet a family not look
through musty papers. I sighed and set to searching for any articles about the incident. "Spring of 1958 is what she said," I thought
as I searched down the pile until I found the 1958 papers. I set
the others aside, pulled up the chair, and began to turn pages. I
looked at stories about businesses, basketball games, town meet-
ings, and every other minor piece of news available in a small
town newspaper.

However, my efforts were rewarded quickly. The paper had
been a weekly paper so there weren't many copies before I got
to the issue of February 13, 1958. In the middle of the front page
was an article titled: *Road Crews Kept Busy Around The Clock
Battling Year's Worst Blizzard*. I quickly read it but there was
no mention of rescued motorists. I took the article out to Mrs.
Robinson.

"Did you find something?" she asked as she saw me coming.

"Yes and no," I replied and handed the newspaper to her.

She looked at it quickly. "Ah, I think this is the storm you
referred to."

"Yes, but there is no mention of any stranded motorists or their being helped. And there is no mention of the Negro family – Jonas, you said?"

"Did you look at the following issues for more news?"

"Ah, no," I said sheepishly.

She looked over her glasses and with no words, I knew what she expected. I returned to the room and looked at more musty papers. After I searched for nearly an hour, Mrs. Robinson came into the room. "How are you doing? Any success?" From my look, she guessed the answer to her question was no. "You have worked hard and I am impressed by the effort you made. Maybe we will have to look at some other sources."

With that she helped me gather up and restack the papers. I took the pile and she showed where they went on the shelf. We proceeded out to her desk.

"I wish I had a way to copy this article for you, but I don't." I shuffled my feet in what I am sure was an impatient way. "Here is some paper. Sit over there and copy the first couple paragraphs. I have an idea that might work."

Again, I was confused and frustrated. However, I did as she asked. It took me about fifteen minutes, and I returned to her desk. "Mrs. Robinson, I do appreciate your help, but I would really like to meet this family. Would you please give me directions?"

Mrs. Robinson looked squarely at me this time, stood and took my hand in hers. "Ron, you have shown me you are very committed to your search. You also seem to be a gentle person who means no harm. I do not want you to think unkindly of me but this is what I propose to do. My husband and Mr. Jonas are good friends so we will stop by their house soon. I will show him this article, explain what you are doing, and ask if it is ok to send you to see him. What do you think of that?"

"But Mrs. Robinson do you have to go to all that trouble? I only…"

She held up her finger again to hush me. "I know you are in a hurry. But history has scared this family in many ways. I want to be very sensitive to their feelings. I would hope you could understand that and be patient."

I felt her warmness as she held my hand. I felt I could trust her. I nodded my agreement.

"Good," she said. "When can you meet me here again? I know you work in a store. Is this your regular day off?"

"Yes," I replied with a noticeable sadness in my voice.

She patted my hand and said, "OK, I will see you next week Tuesday and we'll see where we go from there."


I left for Mancelona the following Tuesday with high expectations. I was waiting at the library when Mrs. Robinson arrived to work. She waved to me, went in a rear door, and disappeared. Soon she was opening the front door and motioned for me to come inside.

"You are here early today! It is good to see you again,"

I was anxious to get to the point. "Did you talk to Mr. Jonas?"

"Oh yes we had a wonderful visit a couple nights ago. He and my husband are working on another job starting tomorrow in fact. It is good you came today because Jonas is most likely home. Do you want those directions now?"

"Yes, I am so grateful for your help."

"Yes, we live just another half-mile north of Jonas and on the same side of the highway. Do you want me to draw a map?"

"No, I am pretty familiar with the area, but thank you for offering."

"Go north about eight miles on the four-lane highway to where the road curves to the left. There is a turnaround there, and that turnaround is right in line with Jonas's driveway. You'll find it easily. If you miss that crossover, the four-lane ends in about a half-mile, and then you're at our driveway. You could turn around there; it says 'Robinson' on the box. You can't miss it."

"Oh, thank you, thank you." I reached out and shook her hand. I was in a hurry and began to rush out. I stopped, still holding the door. "Excuse me, ma'am. What is Jonas's last name?"

"His name is 'Jonas Lewis Jackson.' He is always proud to tell anyone. Others call him by a nasty name I will not repeat."

"No, I won't either, ma'am!"

"Here take your copy of the article. I showed it to Jonas and maybe he will trust you more if you have it when you arrive. Good luck!"

# 15 - Visiting

*I was a mixture of feelings*

*My thoughts were a blur.*

*My fears crept in as I started*

*But fear or not, excited was for sure.*

*Up the road I flew*

*Like I already knew,*

*But the surprises ahead*

*Were going to be far more than just new.*

Soon I was hurrying north, and as the road curved, there was a crossover, just as Mrs. Robinson had said. The sign read *For Emergency Vehicles Only*, but there was not a car in sight, so I turned. As she had said, there was a dirt driveway and an old mailbox. There was no name on the box, but I assumed I was where I wanted to be and slowly drove in the drive. It was not well-worn—more of a two-track—and I could not see a house until I passed the big maple shading or maybe shielding the place. It was hard to notice the house in the shadiness of the big trees, for it was covered in black paper with lath strips nailed regularly. My dad always referred to those houses disparagingly as "tar paper shacks." I

could see several outbuildings but no vehicle, so I stopped short of
the house and sat there observing for a moment.

Flowers always make a house in any condition a real home. I
noticed some in pots near a side door and another row along some
stones laid like a walk. But no people came out.

All of a sudden, I felt a bit of panic. What would I tell this family if I did meet them? "Hi, I'm a white kid who wants to meet a
Negro"? Now I was beginning to feel like a fool. But if I'd gotten
this far, I wasn't stopping now, and I got out of the car.

I hadn't taken but two or three steps when a man appeared
around the back corner of the house. He stopped and just looked
at me.

"Hi!" I said, and I waved and smiled. I was sure I didn't look
threatening with my father's big old station wagon.

"What ch'ya sellin'? Whatever 'tis, I's don't need none! Get
on now!" He waved me to leave. "Now git and leave an old feller
be!" he said in a firm tone. He reached down, picked up something
from near the house, and walked away. He disappeared around the
house and I was left standing there. What should I do? I was smart
enough to know the big *No Trespassing* sign could mean business.
That is the way people get shot and it was not going to be me.

I turned to go and heard what I thought to be the squeak of a
door. I turned toward the house, but I didn't see anybody.

By the time I got back to my car, I had decided to leave a note.
I addressed it formally to *Mr. Jonas Jackson*, and explained Mrs.
Robinson had sent me to meet his family. I told him I hoped we

could talk if I came back the following evening, and signed my name. I folded it together with my copy of the newspaper article Mrs. Robinson had given back to me. I looked for where to put the note, and decided not to go up to the door. Instead, I attached it to a clip on the mailbox, and hoped he would find it there.

There was nothing left to do but to leave. I pulled out and headed back toward town. I felt odd like I had never felt before. Did Mr. Jonas not like me? I was shocked not having him accept my friendliness. I rolled these new feelings around in my head all the way home.

After work the next evening, I drove back to Jonas's house. When I drove up Jonas was digging near the flowers I had admired at my first visit. He stood up, just looking at me as I got out and walked toward him.

"You's still a trying ta sell Mr. Jonas somethin'?"

"No, nothing for sale, sir. Ah, Mrs. Robinson told me how to find your place." I walked a couple steps closer.

"You's mean ma neighbor, Mrs. Robinson?"

"Yes, I met her at the library in town."

He didn't move, but he did seem to soften some; he took off his well-worn hat and scratched his head. He took a couple steps toward me and then said, "Yousa got some work for ole' Jonas!"

I was taken aback by the singsong way he said that, kind of like the lines in that minstrel show. I did not reply. He took a couple steps closer.

"If'n you's got work, Jonas here's your man, sir."

That "sir" hurt me more, for I was nineteen years old and he was well my senior; it sounded so wrong.

"I's can build or cut wood or dig or haul. My ol' truck yonder still workin' good."

I held up my hands to stop his pleas. "No, no, I just had a couple questions. That's all."

All of a sudden, his facial expression went from a half-toothless grin to serious worry. "Is you's one of dem investigators? Always sneakin' 'round tryin' to get ole' Jonas here in a heap o' trouble."

"Mr. Jonas, my father told me of the snowstorm. I understand from Mrs. Robinson it was in 1958. He spoke about your wonderful, gracious help to those stranded folks."

I watched Jonas closely for any reaction. So far I'd only gotten about six feet from my car; Jonas had equally only come about six feet from the corner of his house. We were facing off like two opposing forces, and I hated the feeling. I was surprised in my naive way at Jonas's hesitancy and mistrust. I'd never felt like I was the enemy before, and it did not feel good at all. So as Jonas shifted his feet he suddenly smiled.

"Oh, ya, we's had a house full dat night!" He laughed. I nodded and smiled in agreement. "You say your daddy tolt you da story?"

"Yes, I think you might know my dad. He says you and your wife have come to our farm to buy apples in the past years."

"Is your daddy Mr. Carl? Well, I'll be! How's come I's never seen you at da apples?"

"I guess because I was away at school by the time apple harvest came."

"Oh, yes, in college, eh? Your daddy must be mighty proud of ya, son. You workin' hard?"

"Yes, sir!" I liked that I could return the "sir" and point respect in the proper direction.

"You know's, your daddy only one got's them Cortland's, and they's the only apple my lady uses for sauce."

But as we took a few steps closer to each other, both literally and figuratively, Jonas's brow wrinkled again, and he put his hat back on. He reached down and picked up a handful of boards.

"Well, I's got work to do. Nice of you to stop. Tell Mr. Carl we be seein' him in da fall."

He then turned to walk away, but then several of the boards slipped off his arm. One of them knocked off his hat and I thought maybe hit his head. Instinctively, I stepped up and grabbed the teetering boards.

"No need, sonny. Jonas can do OK his self."

I picked up one board that had dropped. I stood there look-ing at it with, I was sure, my mouth wide open. Jonas noticed my surprise.

"What ya lookin' at, sonny?"

I turned the board toward Jonas and pointed to the branded letters on the board.

"What you's know about 'Bound for Glory'?" he asked.

Again my mouth dropped, and I stammered for words.

"Do you, that is…I've not heard of 'Bound for Glory,' but does the name Colonel Benning mean anything to you?"

Jonas looked at me, into me, and through me like I'd never felt anyone do before. It was as if he could see inside me, and I felt a bit of a shiver.

"Maybe it's does, and maybe it's don't," was all he said.

I handed him the board and stepped back so as not to appear at all threatening. That in and of itself was a laugh. I'm only five feet six inches tall, weigh about 135 pounds, and have curly blond hair. Threatening was not a trait I ever had. However, I knew my mere presence was somehow threatening to Mr. Jonas.

"Mr. Jonas, sir, could I come back another day and show you some things I've found? My friend Jack, back at Clam River, showed me a board identical to that one several weeks ago. He's the one who mentioned the name Benning, and I've done some research on his Civil War record. He was a colonel in the Union army. Please, may I return and share some things with you?"

Jonas stood transfixed with his eyes locked on mine. I imagined if he hadn't been holding the boards he'd have again taken off his hat and scratched his head. Finally, he spoke.

"Son, you's got a gentle soul. I's can see it. Bring back your information. We'll talk some."

"Thank you, Mr. Jonas, sir. My next day off work is next Tuesday. This is Thursday, and that would be five days away. Would that be OK?"

He didn't speak; he just nodded, turned, and disappeared around the back corner of the house from where he'd originally appeared. I turned to leave and noticed the screen door pull shut and the curtain ripple. I had the feeling we had not been alone during this conversation. I returned to the car quickly and left.

My heart was pounding when I jumped out at the library and ran up the short stairs to the door. I again disturbed the peaceful quiet so important to librarians, I was afraid Mrs. Robinson would shush me with her finger. I was pleased when she broke into a big smile as I appeared at her desk.

"Well, young man, judging by your grin, I'm guessing you had some success? Did you find Jonas?"

"Yes, I did, and we agreed to meet again Tuesday, my next day off, so I could show him some things from my friend Jack and some of the research I've—"

"Hold it! Hold it!" she interrupted and cut me off. "Slower, please. Did you talk to Jonas about the storm?"

"Well, that is only the beginning, ma'am. Yes, we did do that some, and I also found out he buys apples from my father's orchard; I think that was what softened him up."

"Softened him up?" she asked.

"Yes, no offense meant, but Mr. Jonas was very reluctant to trust me and kept his distance."

She sort of sighed and dropped her head, and a deeply concerned expression appeared on her face.

"Ron—it was Ron, correct?" I nodded, and she went on. "You're too young to understand; on the other hand, I guess I've never understood, and I'm a good bit older…not all that old, mind you." Her eyes glimmered, and a slight coy smile showed. "You have to understand not all people like Jonas or even think he should live here at all. There have been incidents, and we've always tried to be good neighbors, but sometimes I'm not sure they truly trust us because we are just 'white folk.'"

"White folk?" I said it with a strange feeling and let it slide off my tongue like I tasted some new vegetable for the first time and didn't like it. "Mrs. Robinson, Jonas acknowledged you were a good and I think trusted neighbor. I apologize if I 'dropped your name' and it helped him trust me a tiny bit, but we're going to meet next Tuesday, and I'm going to bring some work I've been studying, specifically about a Civil War veteran who it seems might be connected not only to Clam but also somehow to Mr. Jonas."

Mrs. Robinson added with equal interest, "Oh, there were quite a few Civil War veterans who moved into our North Country after the war. Some came to receive land grants for their service; some were from the area, and others had come maybe just to get far away from the war. Do you have a specific person or event you're researching?"

"Sort of. You see, it started when I took a history course on the Civil War last year at school. The teacher was all about the 'people in the war,' not just the battles, and we wrote a paper at the end. The professor had put a bunch of info on hold at the library, and I became especially interested in some diaries that were there. They were so personal and so tender on both sides. But before that my friend Jack over in Clam had brought up the name Benning in connection to Clam River. He had a shipping business, and there is a road with his name. So, I also tried to research his name, and I was excited to find some info and a part of his diary. His name was Colonel Matthew Benning, and he was assigned to the Michigan Brigade, either the Fifth or Sixth Cavalry. There were many units from Michigan. So that is about all I know, so far."

I had not noticed Mrs. Robinson making a note on her desk paper as we talked. She asked, "Benning Road is over by Alden, isn't it?"

"Yes, same one, I'm sure. The story ends because the diary was found on his dead horse, and no body was recovered. He was recorded as being killed in the Battle of the Wilderness in May of 1864."

I took a quick look at my watch and noticed the day had flown by. I had commitments in the evening and needed to rush. I quickly gathered up my notes, thanked Mrs. Robinson, and rushed out to my car. I sat in the parking lot for a minute, composing some thoughts and making some notes. What troubled me most was to be thought of as "white folk" as well as the idea that I could be threatening to an obviously kindhearted Negro man. I had never felt anyone didn't like me or didn't trust me. Could someone even hate me? How could that be?

# 16 - Crossing Stories

*I raced back to Clam, my head still in a blur.*

*Needed to share the BFG news for sure.*

*Oh, where is this going?*

*Oh, how could stories cross?*

*Should I stop here or go on?*

*What would be the loss?*

*I know a sage will help me sort*

*The details out and see the direction of my report.*

*I'm back to the Clam, glad the sage there resides.*

*My mind is a blur. So much I don't know inside.*

I headed back to Clam in a rush to share with Jack. I checked my watch and determined Jack would have probably just finished his dinner, which he usually had around five. I had lots of ideas rolling in my head and do not recall anything about the ten-mile trip, but I was brought to attention as I turned off the main road toward Clam. There I saw the police car parked at Jack's driveway. No lights were flashing, but I was certainly confused, so I quickly stopped the car behind the cruiser. As I ran around the cruiser to the driveway, I was even more concerned when I found an emergency ambulance vehicle in the drive by the porch.

I ran past the ambulance to the steps just as one of the workers came out of the house. I knew him as a classmate from my high school days.

"Oh, Ron," he said in surprise. "Are you a relative?"

"No," I replied somewhat breathlessly, "just a friend. But how is Jack? Is he OK?"

He smiled and replied, "Yes, he's OK. A false alarm. You'll be able to see him in a few minutes. Wait out here. There's not enough room in that small cottage. Excuse me. I need something from the van." He hurried off.

I did as directed and moved to sit on the edge of the porch out of the way. As I went over by the chairs, I heard a sound and noticed One-Eyed Jack—the cat—hiding from all the chaos under one of the chairs. I sat on the edge of the porch and was nearly at eye level with him (and his one eye). Jack the cat saw me and appeared from under the chair. He approached me. He rubbed my hand, and I was sure he had to be scared or at best confused by all the people hurrying around.

Jack had never explained the cat's presence, but I concluded he might just be a stray. I guess the two lost souls sort of bonded. I wondered if he went home with Jack to Cassopolis. I'm sure he had to because Jack spoke of finding him there.

The cat began to purr, and I could also hear some of the conversation from inside.

I heard Jack say sternly, "Oh, I'm OK. You don't have to take me anywhere!"

One of the EMTs responded, "I know, Mr. Jackson, but when you didn't respond to your daughter's calls, she requested the sheriff come and see. Officer Jim could not get an answer at the door but could see you slumped in your chair, so he called us."

"I know, I know, but now, you understand, a man can't even have a good nap without being bothered!"

"No bother, Mr. Jackson. Don't be too hard on your daughter; I'm sure she's just worried."

"Yeah, like a mother hen!" Jack mumbled. I laughed at Jack's stubbornness.

"Please don't leave the phone off the hook again either; that just made her worry more."

"Yeah, yeah, you're all like mother hens! I just bumped the thing; that's all."

"Well, Mr. Jackson, all your vitals are OK, and you have stayed on the doctor's medications, haven't you?"

"Oh, yes, yes, and I carry those stupid little yellow ones here in my pocket somewhere!"

"Please, not 'somewhere,' Mr. Jackson. Keep them close. They could keep you from having another spell."

"Yes! Yes!" I was listening closely, but I could only discern that Jack had some condition with his heart. My dad had something similar, and I remembered the "little yellow pills." I hoped it wasn't serious, but obviously Jack didn't care to talk about it. I would try to honor that and not pester him. I didn't think he needed another "mother hen."

The two ambulance guys that I assumed were EMTs came out with their bags. Eddie, the one I knew, came over to me.

"He sure is a cantankerous old guy, isn't he? How'd you two become friends?"

"Oh, that's a long story. It started because I've been down here working over at the store all the time the last two summers."

Eddie nodded and added, "Is Dave still working there? We graduated together. I'll have to stop over."

"I appreciate you being here and taking care of the old man."

Eddie leaned close to me. "He's got to be careful; he's not real healthy." About then his partner honked the horn to get his attention.

I heard a voice from behind me as the screen door squeaked.

"Who you callin' an old man?"

My friend smiled, said bye to Jack, and jumped in the van. They backed out quickly and left.

"Well, don't just sit there like a bump; come and help me to my chair."

I jumped up and held the door. I thought Jack did look a bit more frail. With the cane in one hand, he took my arm to steady himself. We made the few feet to the chair, and he sat with a *plop*. He breathed his patented sigh and closed his eyes.

Although I had learned to be patient during silence, I was more worried now. I sat forward after some long moments and was about to touch his arm or shake him when he spoke.

"Darn daughter, calling the cops! I'll be darned, and just because I bumped the phone off the hook! Mother hen, and I say it again, I don't need it!"

I wisely chose not to respond but just listened. I settled back in the chair and waited. After a couple of minutes, he spoke again.

"You not workin' today? Remember you've got to keep payin' that social security for me." And then he chuckled.

Whatever his health problem was, he sure had a great spirit and never seemed to lose his sense of humor. I loved that about him and made a mental note to be sure I was the same when I got older.

"Yes, I had the day off. Can I tell you what I did?"

"Sure, it's been lonesome around here today. I was so bored I took the phone off the hook just to get some company to come and see me!"

We both laughed at that incredible spirit of his.

"Remember I told you I've been struggling with that minstrel show thing? I had a long talk with my dad, and he shared a story about a Negro family that lives over near Mancelona. They helped some people during a blizzard in 1958. The long and the short of it is I went over and looked them up today."

"Oh, are they still living in the area? I'm surprised." Jack seemed a bit more attentive as I went on.

"Yes, I found the man, and his name is Jonas, Jonas Lewis Jackson to be exact!"

"Jackson? Maybe we're related?" Jack peeked at me with one squinted eye and smiled, and I groaned at his bad joke.

"What was most interesting to me—and actually most troubling, too—was that he was friendly but in a distant, untrusting way. I've never felt anyone did not trust me. I felt like he was afraid I might…"

"Might what, son? Might hurt him like probably lots of dumb, prejudiced white folk have over the years?"

I grimaced again. "There's that phrase 'white folk' again! I've never thought of myself as 'white folk'! That makes me feel like I'm the enemy, like I'm the Klan or something."

"Well, son, you're plenty young and have lots to learn, but those are surely 'white folk' under those Klan hoods, not Negroes. Sounds like you learned a lot today. Good for you. Actually, I'm impressed you were so gutsy to go there."

"Well, thanks, and I'm going back. Mr. Jonas agreed to meet with me next Tuesday, which is my next day off."

"Have you got a look at that book I gave you on the Underground Railroad?"

"Not much. I just leafed through the first chapter or so."

"Say then, you go inside and grab that other book on the table and bring it out here."

As I crawled out of the chair, I nearly stepped on Jack the cat, who scooted in the door when I opened it. I returned with a book and read the title: *The History of Cassopolis, and Their Part in the Underground Railroad*. Then I handed it to Jack.

"I've been reading this off and on. My daughter got this for me along with the other one. I guess she worried I'd get bored up here. Point is, many folk here in Michigan were involved in transporting slaves and former slaves out of the South and on to Canada and freedom."

"Why all the way to Canada? Wasn't slavery outlawed in Michigan?"

"Yes, that is true, but there was some act of Congress that said that bounty hunters could come into northern states and drag slaves back to their former owners. They made good money doing that. Therefore, the former slaves were not safe until they got clear to Canada."

"That's new to me—oh, I've heard of the Underground Railroad and the freeing of slaves, just not about Michigan's part in it or the bounty hunters. I need to do more research on that. I'm going to take a course this fall called Literature of the Civil Rights Movement. Now I'm even more interested."

Our conversation came to a pause, and Jack leafed through some of the book.

"I want to ask Jonas to tell me about the storm incident. I thought that would help him know I meant no harm. He softened a bit when he connected me to my dad because he and his wife come over to our orchard to buy apples every fall."

"You're right, and that is a mature way to help the man feel at ease with you. Just remember he does not owe you respect; you owe him respect."

I locked eyes with Jack and remembered Jonas looking straight at me similarly. Jack seemed to have the same ability to see deep inside me. I hope he liked what he saw.

"Mr. Jonas looked at me just like you're doing now, like he could see deep inside. Then he said, 'Son, you have a gentle soul. I can see it.' And then he agreed that I could come back next Tuesday."

Jack smiled, and we sat pondering it all, listening to the night. The sun was setting, and we heard a loon again. What a sound, and what a feeling that sound seemed to stir in me.

"I'm going to miss that sound." At least, that's what I thought I heard Jack mutter to no one in particular. I was too scared to ask what he meant.

✿

# 17 - Mother's Brownies

*Is getting old scary?*

*Why does this man's frailty scare me so?*

*We all know we all will go,*

*But Jack and his shack are no*

*Simple place, but where I've gone to find a face,*

*To find an ear, to hear the quiet of the place.*

*No clue to know what it all means.*

*I'm confused, but it doesn't seem*

*To be an end; maybe I'm just green.*

*I'll grow and change. I always know*

*I'm goin' home to brownies, so there I go.*

Jack seemed tired, and I asked him if I could help him into the house. I was surprised when he agreed and gave me his hand to help pull him up. He teetered for a moment and then got his balance, and I opened the screen door.

"Good night, son!" was all he said.

When I got home, my mother was fussing in the kitchen. She turned to me immediately and handed me a note off the table.

"This lady called here just before five and said she was hoping you'd call her back. I was sure you were working or busy with something else. She said to be sure to tell you she had found something you would be very interested in, and she emphasized that 'very' several times."

"Wow, that is so exciting!"

"What is this all about?"

"Well, I don't know where to start, but I've got to work tomorrow all day."

I guess my mother sensed I was thinking out loud about how to find time to get to the Mancelona Library, and she spoke up, interrupting my confused thoughts.

"Maybe I can help. Let me tell you, son, you must have really impressed Mrs. Robinson today. She was very complimentary and went on and on about the 'nice young man' she had just met."

We both laughed as I puffed out my chest. "And what did you expect?" We both laughed again.

"Well, so here's my offer. I was planning to go shopping for food over there tomorrow. Mrs. Robinson knows me from school. I'm sure she'd let me check out whatever this is for you. What do you think of that?"

"That would be great! I'm really anxious to see what she's found. I hope it's about Colonel Benning."

"Who is Colonel Benning?"

"Like I said, it's a long story."

"I'm not going anywhere. Are you? I've got fresh brownies to coax you into telling me more."

"It's a deal."

As we sat at the kitchen table, I told Mom the lengthy story, including about Jack, his cottage at Clam River, and his one-eyed cat. I shared my struggles with the minstrel show. I told her what Dad had said about the snowstorm and my decision to find this family for myself.

"I met Mrs. Robinson at the library. I went there to get some help in finding this family. As it turned out, she and her husband are neighbors of this Negro family. She was hesitant and somewhat protective of them, but she agreed to check with the family to see if it was ok. I went back later and she gave me directions. The man's name is Jonas Lewis Jackson, and I haven't met his wife. But I'm going back for another visit on Tuesday. Mom, since I went to the university, things just don't look the same as they did growing up here. Don't take that wrong; it's just so much bigger!"

"Son, you and your world will always be bigger than that of your father's and mine. My world expanded when I went away to the university, and that was thirty years ago! I'm proud and excited for what you're growing into and becoming. You keep it up."

I could see wetness building in her eyes and felt that it was probably building in mine, too. We both fumbled a bit, and then, in her favorite way, she rescued us from our uncomfortable situation.

She said, "Here, have another brownie!" I gladly took one. "However," she went on, "that doesn't explain 'Colonel Benning.'"

"I don't know where to start there, either, and I also don't quite know how it connects. Jack told me about how his father had married a daughter of the man who owned the store way back around the turn of the century. They were especially active during the time of Prohibition. Apparently, according to a book I found about the Torch Lake area, there was no shortage of booze around this area. Jack claims his father was one of the chief bootleggers and Anderson's bar was the center of the business. According to his father, they smuggled the booze in large shipping crates that came in on steamers and were unloaded at Clam River to lighten the ships. The booze would be removed from the large shipping containers, and then the regular merchandise would be distributed on up the North Country by wagon and rail. There were a lot of small settlements and lumber mills to be supplied."

My mother looked perplexed as she struggled to take this all in. "Yes, I will get to Benning soon!" I assured her. "Benning was a Civil War veteran who came to the area as a pioneer after the war. He set up this shipping business in the area of Clam. Anderson married his daughter and took it over after the colonel died. I'm not sure about when exactly all those things happened. I hope Mrs. Robinson has found some information to help with that. But there is another very confusing piece of information I just found today. The name of the company was Benning Freight Goods, and it had a logo that was an oval with *BFG* in the middle. Jack showed me lots of packing boards at his cottage with that logo branded on them. Now here is the mysterious part. When I was in Mancelona today and met Jonas, he happened to pick up some boards. One of them dropped, and I picked it up for him. It had the same *BFG* brand on it! Now I believe there is some connection between the two stories, and I plan to figure it out if it takes me all summer to do it."

My mother was quiet, and I couldn't tell if she was lost, overwhelmed, or concerned. She fussed with our dirty glasses and put them in the sink.

"You telling me all this adventure has been going on right here in little ol' Clam River?"

"It would seem so! That's enough of the story for tonight."

We bid each other good-night, and I went out into the backyard. It was very dark, and a breeze was blowing. I walked down the stairs to the circle drive in front of the house to retrieve the book. Just as I picked it out of the bike's saddlebag, I heard something. I stopped and listened closely, but there were no more noises.

I turned to walk back and heard it again. We were too far from the lake to hear boats or loons. Maybe the wind was whistling around our house in some odd way. I walked to the backyard and sat at the table. I opened the book to the table of contents. I could read it pretty well by the light of our back door, and I scanned through it.

My finger stopped at chapter 11, the title of which jumped out at me. It was "Bound for Glory and Other Songs." Hadn't Jonas mentioned that song?

There was that sound again. Was it a moan, a groan, a wail, or just my overzealous imagination? I thought I'd better get some rest.

# 18 - Returning

*I'm goin' back to a daring place.*

*It is not scary; I find it full of quiet grace.*

*Why would others fear?*

*Why would they not cheer*

*The helpful open door*

*With the warm and open hearth?*

*Come in you weary whose way is bleary!*

*How can that be?*

*Those others would see*

*A threatening thing among the gold*

*When one reaches out, young or old.*

Tuesday came quickly, and the sun broke it open brightly. That was a good sign. I was anxious about my day and yet looking forward to seeing a new friend again. I had my notes, and I had my board I'd borrowed from Jack. Jack was excited with me, too, as we shared this adventure together. The mystery of the board was like a link between us.

I had not thought much about this whole experience until I was at Jack's and he got the board for me. So much of our friendship was like passing something on to me like they do in relay races. He was the sage and passed on wisdom to me. I was the open book on whom he could write and pass on his life learning. Now this board with the mysterious *BFG* was literally acting like a baton. As he passed it to me, I felt I now had possession of not only his wisdom but also part of his history or even, you could say, his very life. I felt a part of something much larger than myself, than his or my friendship, than my learning to love and respect others who are different from myself, than old, dusty history coming alive right here in my life, than anything I could have imagined for my quiet summer working in the Clam. I packed the board and got into the car. I drove on into something big.

I found myself nearly at Jonas's house before hardly realizing it. I reminded myself that I'd better write down some of this heavy stuff tonight.

I turned into the drive and found Jonas cutting weeds along it, by the house to the main road. He acknowledged me with a nod but never lost the rhythm of his cutting. I pulled up short of the house under the big maple and watched him. He reminded me of my grandfather as he made steady swings back and forth, creating perfectly even cuts. He was using a scythe just like I remembered my grandfather using years ago. Going back and forth with even cuts required that the blade be perfectly sharp. My grandfather used to stop, flip the scythe blade up, and pull a whetstone from his hip pocket. He'd then hone that blade with a blur of strokes going back and forth. I'd often tried to imitate that skill, but I had never come close.

Skills like this are nearly extinct, so I was blessed to see a man at one with his tools, applying a skill I'd never possessed but could admire deeply as I saw it in action. He moved down and around the mailbox and stopped. I could see he wasn't done. But I could almost see him say "thems weeds sure be there tomorrow" as he surveyed what he had done and what he had yet to do. He pulled out a red bandanna from his pocket, took off his hat, and wiped his sweaty brow. It was a hot job, and the day was getting pretty warm, even though it was just midmorning. Returning both his hat and the bandanna, he walked over to me as I got out of the car with my backpack in hand.

"Good day, Mr. Jonas!" I said with a grin, and we shook hands. "That looks like hard work! I never could get the rhythm correct and never was very good with a scythe. My dad always accused me of fighting the scythe instead of letting it do its own work."

We walked up the drive a few steps into the shade. Jonas finally acknowledged my greeting and spoke.

"Yoo daddy a wise man."

I had nearly forgotten about what I had said and was confused for a moment about Jonas's comment. He leaned the scythe on the tree and wiped his forehead again.

"You's mentioned the storm last time you's here. Sho' was colder that day! See that there mailbox yonder? It was buried completely. See that fence along da highway? You's couldn't see it t'all. The wind sho piled it up! Dat storm was a pistol!"

I just listened, taking it all in.

"Da first car done got stuck just up yonder past that there drive. Ran into a drift and pulled da car clean into da ditch 'bout by that there tree." He pointed, and I tried to tell exactly where he was pointing.

"Da salesman guy done went into da middle from da other side down there about where's that speed sign is. A neighbor got stuck right there abouts," As he pointed I tried again to follow. Jonas went on. "I think they's musta stopped to help da salesman guy out. No ways they's gonna get back on da road again afta that. They's was almost home too, they's live just up yonder past Robinson's place."

"What about the truck?" I asked, for that was the only part of the story I had heard from my father.

"Yeah, he got stuck too causein' he stopped or at least slowed when dat big Caddy went spinnin' into the ditch yonder. I think he hit da brake so's not to hit her and then just couldn't get dat there big rig a goin' again. He was a special gem of a guy."

With that tour of the storm, Jonas picked up the scythe, and we moved up the drive. We got up near where Jonas and I had talked on our previous visit, and he stopped. I wasn't sure what to do.

"My mom has flowers like these," I said, not knowing what else to do to ease the tension. "She and my dad always love flowers. He grows huge dahlias and loves to pick one and put it in a vase for her." All the time I talked, Jonas, leaning on the scythe, studied me. "Do you plant the flowers?" I finally asked, hinting at getting an answer as to whether there was a wife or anyone else around. Jonas stood his ground, sort of between me and the house. I could feel that lack of trust again and not only did not like it but also had no clue what to do about it. I heard the screen door squeak, followed by a voice.

"Cryin' out loud, Jonas, quit bein' so rude and bring that there nice boy in here for a cold drink. You's be surely need one, too."

I looked up to see a short, ample woman holding the door open. She had the typical full apron that most women wore; my mom had many similar ones. Mostly, I noticed a welcoming smile shine just like the sun did off her glasses. I was mightily relieved.

Jonas's demeanor melted like an ice cube on the pavement.

"This here's the lady of the house, son. This is Mrs. Jackson. Ma, this here is…oh, there I go forgettin'!"

"His name's Ron, Jonas, you old man!"

That comment certainly confirmed my suspicion she had been listening to the conversation the last time. I was sure she could quote it word-for-word!

"Come in here ya' all. I hope's iced tea OK?" She asked and directed us to a small table in the kitchen. I nodded, smiled, and muttered a thank you. I sat down and pushed my backpack under the chair as I surveyed their very humble home.

"You's take sugar, young man? Ma Jonas and me are enough southern we's needs our sugar!" We all smiled, feeling the tension starting to slowly melt like the ice in our glasses. I spoke.

"What do *you* remember about the storm, ma'am?"

Jonas seemed relieved I had taken the pressure off him to say something. Mrs. Jackson stopped her puttering, wiped her hands, and came to sit in the third chair at the table. She smiled as she looked me in the eye. Her eyes smiled with her mouth; I especially liked people who smile all over their faces.

"Oh, son, dat's easy! It was da food. Jonas here had a big ole' wood pile, though they had to keep shovelin' the path as da snow and wind kept a goin' awful all da night long. But food, you see, son, we's humble folk and weren't expectin' no company. Certainly not that group!"

Jonas softened and added, "Yes, Mama here did her best, and all da folk had hot drink to keep 'um warm and got fed, maybe not a lots, but we's didn't starve neither."

Mrs. Jackson continued to recall the story.

"We's all just gathered around, stayin' close to that heatin' stove yonder."

Jonas cut in. "Not enough chairs, so I grabbed two crates from da shed. Maybe they's your daddy's apple boxes! I better check and take them back!" He grinned, and I finally felt the ice had melted, yet the tea was still refreshingly cool.

Mrs. Jackson got up, got the tea pitcher from the refrigerator, and refilled Jonas's and my glasses. We all sat and sipped in the pause, and then Mrs. Jackson spoke up with a soft, reflective voice.

"I does remember one particular happenin' relatin' to the food. Jonas, you 's remember da big lady with da big car?" He nodded, and she went on. "Da lady sho was not happy bein' here, especially here." She raised her eyebrows. "She just sat in that there chair yonder, kept her coat on, and clutchin' that big ole' bag. You's remember dat, Jonas?"

Jonas added, "She di'nt speak. Me and the truck driver nearly had to pull her from da car, she protested so. We's was way too dark for her even before the nighttime came, if you get's what I's meanin'?"

Mrs. Jackson scowled at him for a moment, and after another sip she sighed, seeming to be organizing her thoughts.

"The lady, she's just sat there, and all tried to make her feel at ease. But she's just sat in dat there corner holding tight like to her valise. I didn't notice nothin' special; it was late, and we all were tired, and the conversation was a dying down. Some were dozin'. I was frettin' where everyone might sleep. She got's up and sort of cleared her throat and said somethin' like 'I've got some food here to share,' and she began to pull out things from the bag. It was like a miracle had happened; everyone was stunned for a moment. Then Mary, our neighbor from up the road, got up and helped her. Everyone sort of looked at each other; den we's all seemed to smile at once and shared the food." Mrs. Jackson sat back, seemed to think for a moment, and then spoke in a kind of a hushed tone. "You's know, it was a lot like church, sharin' and all."

That was a profound summation of the depth and miracle of that tense situation in which all had been thrown together by circumstances. In this case something bigger had happened than just sheltering; I can't quite find the words to describe it, but it was surely a miracle.

Jonas continued the story. "It was along nears to noon next day when we's heard da big truck plows a workin' da road. We's hustled to shovel da drive. Ha, I's lent dat salesman guy a big ol' jacket and some buckle boots! He was quite a sight! I's got the tractor out, and we'all shoveled. We's had all dem cars out 'afore dark. Da truck needed a big tow rig, whichn' his company sent from Cadillac, I's believe."

Mrs. Jackson refilled our glasses. I noticed Jonas's face started to look sad, and he took a deep breath and sighed. "Mr. B from the store uptown come and gave us lots of groceries, and da truck showed up with that there new stove. He took our pictures 'for the paper,' he said. But Mr. B came back in about a week with some more groceries and said there'd be no story. Da paper done wouldn't do it. "Dat's not all. I's workin' up at Mr. reedy's farm, and he'd surely heard about da storm and all. He sort of took me aside one day. 'Don't you niggers be gettin' a big head!' he told me, shaking his finger at me. With dat da whole thing ended and been forgotten."

I felt sad. These were such humble, sharing people who were not appreciated much for their gift. Is life like that? Are all Negro people treated that way? I wanted to share this with my friend Lenny at school. I took a note to remind me to do that very thing.

After the conversation quieted down and a new, fresh breeze rippled through the curtains, I noticed the bees working the flowers just outside the door. Mrs. Jackson spoke up.

"What was you's goin'a share 'bout Colonel Benning?"

I was relieved that the conversation was taking a new direction. I reached in my pack and pulled out Jack's board. I showed them the *BFG* branding, and Mrs. Jackson was visibly surprised. She put her hand to her mouth and just shook her head. She slowly rose from her chair, went to the wall by the kitchen window, and pulled back the curtain; there, clear as day, was another identical board with the *BFG* branding on it.

Jonas was in his rocking chair by now and began to hum or sing a song. Mrs. Jackson began to hum as she returned to her chair. Then I heard Jonas sing, "This train is bound for glory, this train."

"You's hush now," she said to him. Then turning to me she said, "Tell us more of what you know, son."

So I shared what little I knew about the colonel. "He started a freight company, and thus there was BFG—Benning Freight Goods."

I noticed she and Jonas exchanged glances as I went on.

"There was a lot of need for shipping of freight in our growing area for the lumbermen and the many small developments dotted all around. Clam River was the perfect place to load and unload freight, some to lighten the boat's load and some to be shipped on to other places."

Again I noticed them exchange glances with no comment.

"My friend Jack, who had this board, lives in a cottage once owned by Benning or his son-in-law Anderson, who had the store at the river in later years. Jack showed me a tunnel in the basement where the Andersons apparently stored the booze they smuggled into the area during Prohibition."

I paused and was about to ask for their reaction when again I noticed them sharing glances. There seemed to be something electric in the air. I could sense it but not name it and probably just sat there with a dumb look on my face.

Jonas spoke first. He cleared his throat and fussed with his glasses as if thinking hard about what to say. He finally faced me and spoke softly.

"Son, you's a good feller with a good soul as I's told you before. There's so much you're a learnin', and there's so much you 's don't know. I's got to go do some work now at another farm. I's be appreciatin' you comin' back another day with all's you wrote and discovered. We'll talk more." Then, he added, "We's got some things you need to see."

# 19 - The Storm

*My mind raced on*

*Like the storm had earlier raged.*

*I felt this family's warmth*

*And the blessing they displayed.*

*Where was this all going?*

*BFG — means many things.*

*Maybe for me it may be simply,*

*The new struggle it will bring.*


My mind raced with the story the Jacksons had shared with me about the storm. I was excited to have them share. I was blessed to have them invite me into their lives. I felt I needed to help tell their story somehow and I first needed to get it written down.

When I got home, I got out my notes and spread them on the kitchen table. I was grateful my parents were gone somewhere. I sat there alone and tried to organize my information. I wanted to share this with Jack but worried his family might be there. I didn't want to interrupt him "so first things first" I reminded myself and began to piece together the story I had been told. I was moved at how sensitive Jonas and his wife had been as they shared. As I think is often true of heroes, they were very humble. They did not feel they had given so much but instead had received so much in return.

I wrote and rewrote for several hours until I felt I had the story clear. I was amazed that some of their story seemed to come out in verse. Again that brought me back to Jack. He had written some poems and I felt he could help me understand. I decided to take a chance. I gathered up my notes, and the story with the poems. I drove down to Clam River in the hopes that Jack was not busy.

I was relieved as I rounded the corner and turned toward the lake, there was no car in his driveway. I pulled in, parked my bike, and walked up to the porch. There were some beach toys in a pile by the steps. A clothes line had been strung from a porch post to the tree and was draped with swim suits. No one seemed to be there. I checked my watch. It was well past dinner time but Jack seemed to be alone in his favorite chair. He was there and Jack, the cat, was curled on his lap. They both seemed to be napping in the quiet evening coolness. The cat roused as I approached and jumped down coming over to me. That roused Jack and he rubbed his eyes yawning. He spoke up, "Well, look who's here. Didn't think I'd be seeing you for a while."

"I hope I'm not butting in. I can see you've got some company." I nodded toward the line of swim suits.

"Oh yes. I got some relief this afternoon for they all went into Traverse City to shop. Come on and sit a spell."

"I hoped I could see you and share about the meeting with the Jacksons. Jonas had to go to work this afternoon so I came home early. I had to sit down and write what they told me of the storm and their interesting guests. I wanted to share it with you as soon as possible."

"I'm glad you came over, son. This bunch here wears me out, so I was just resting a bit. I'm thirsty so let me get us some ice tea. That ok for you?" I nodded as he pulled himself up and went inside the cabin. "Get your stuff out. I'll be right there," he yelled from inside. I heard the clink of glasses and the refrigerator open and close.

I jumped up and held the door as he began to come back out to the porch. "Here, take this tray. I'm not steady enough tonight."

I took the tray while Jack (the man) came out and Jack (the cat) went in. We sat again. I sipped while Jack seemed to need to catch his breath. He looked at me and said, "So you had some adventure today, eh?"

"I don't know quite how to begin but I wanted to share what I wrote." I handed Jack the three pages I'd written.

He reached for his glasses on the stand by the wall.

"When did you get those things?"

"Oh, quit with the old foggy stuff and let me read." With a snort he began to look over the writing. I sat back, sipped my tea, and waited. I noticed the lake was rather quiet tonight. The sun was starting to set and the shadows were lengthening. I saw the 'V' of a loon's wake but heard no familiar call.

Jack spoke. "They must be some fine folk to help so many when they have so little. I am certainly impressed."

"There were five guests and the two of them. If you could see their house, it's barely as big as your cabin. I'd say it's smaller in fact. It must have been a tight fit."

Jack looked up at me from his reading. He smiled and said, "How about the poetry part? Did you catch that from me?" His eyes twinkled as he grinned and we laughed together.

"I wanted to ask you about that," I said.

"About what?"

"I was surprised by the poetry. It was something real new to me. It just came out that way."

Jack sighed and showed his patented sage smirk, took off his glasses and said, "Poems sometimes are ways to express deeper feelings when regular words don't seem to make it. I think I could say things to Em in a poem that I couldn't say in a conversation." He laid his head back, looked out to the water as if he was having a melancholy remembrance of some event. He sighed again, put on his glasses and returned to my writing.

"Take this part here," he said, and he read,

'The mystery remains over the years
All together, so different but there alone.
For barriers, jobs, backgrounds and colors
There in this place, not worth a hill of bones.'

He did not say anything for some moments, sipped some tea and then spoke, "You have tried to say something more than just words. You're digging down deeper, some place near you heart, I think."

I was so moved by what Jack said. I could not respond. We sat in our now customary silence. We both watched the lake as the sunset neared. I could not see the loon's wake but the loon's call came clearly as if right on cue. We both looked at each other and smiled.

Jack looked at my papers again for a while. Then he read again,

'Could they hug? Why not, this is a new day.
The lady of means was the first to say
I speak for us all, can't thank you enough
Without you and your home we'd not be here today.'

"This is a new day" Jack repeated reflectively. "Son, I think you're going to help us see that yet. Times they are a changing."

My ears perked up for those were words of a popular folk song. I must have seemed amazed and Jack must have noticed.

"What? You don't think I listen to the radio?"

We chuckled again at each other. I spoke up, "Thank you for reading this tonight. You're right. I do feel something deeper than I've known before. I know there is more; I just don't know what it is."

Jack handed me back the papers. He fished out his pipe, scratched a match that lit up his face in the darkness. It was a wise face and I thought again how much I appreciated him. "Read me that last part about the end. I think you really had a point there."

I shuffled the papers. "You mean where it starts, 'so how does it end?'?"

"Yes that's it."

The smell of his aromatic pipe smoke seemed the perfect background as I read:

'So how does it end?
Guess it's up to you and me.
There was never a news report
Written or shared for the world to see
And get a glimpse of a miracle that had shown
That night in the swirl of the snow and the wind that was blown.
But there was still more happening there,
In the breaking of barriers; A peek over the wall.
Giving hope maybe one day we'll be able to love one and all.'

"I like that," Jack said softly.

# 20 - Oral History

*It is so good that some people of books*

*Choose to treasure and keep*

*Lost information available for other's looks.*

*Even in this small town with so few around,*

*They have a rich history, and in their record*

*You find those lives that can be relived and rebound.*

*I am one of those who has been let in to glimpse*

*Into the life, the times we've not seen since.*

*Nothing was civil way back then; some came to the land*

*And tried to forget or repent around the River Clam.*

My mother picked up the info at the library, and returning from work, I found a manila folder on the kitchen table with my name on it. I pulled out a handful of papers. On the top of the stack was a letter and then an unbound packet of twenty or so pages with a colored sheet on the top with the title:

## Colonel Matthew Benning – An Oral History

### Narrated by Bella (Benning) Anderson, His Daughter.

### Printed: May 16, 1952.

I laid aside the packet and read the letter first. It said:

August 8, 1964

Dear Mr. Robotham,

("A bit formal," I thought.)

> I believe I have found a piece which will greatly enhance your
> research. Do find enclosed the copy I discovered. I am glad to
> release this through your dear mother into your kind and careful
> possession. I am sure you do understand how valuable this piece is.

(Now I was almost scared to touch it. I thought I'd better be especially careful—I'd better not just stuff it in my pack or my bike's
saddlebag. She writes very formally like I would expect a librarian
to do!)

> I believe I mentioned that my friend, the previous library
> director, did a lot of work collecting Civil War stories. She
> had tried to get oral histories from many. She had started
> this when she first came to the library in the thirties. Most
> of the veterans were dead by then, so most of her informa-
> tion came through families she contacted through the GAR
> (Grand Army of the Republic). You may be able to find more

information for your research and study by contacting them directly.

(I took a note on my calendar to do just that in the fall. It was a good suggestion.)

I do hope this is helpful. The author, Mrs. Anderson, is also deceased now, making this piece, her writing, that much more valuable. I would like you to return it to me in one week. Do be careful.

Thank you for letting me serve you through the Mancelona Library.

Signed, respectfully,

Mrs. B. Robinson, Library Director


I guess *library director* was a more impressive title than just *librarian*, even if there was still only one person working there. I chuckled to myself. I certainly was not making fun of her, though, for she had been very gracious and helpful. I was anxious to read what she had found, and no one seemed to be home here, so no one would bother me if I began now. I sat in the comfy corner chair, switched on the light, opened the cover sheet, and read.


*The Story of My Father's Life by Belle (Benning) Anderson*

My father was born in Hillsdale County, Michigan, in 1838. Like most people his parents, my grandparents, were pioneer farmers. Their names were Matthew Sr. and Isabella. I am blessed to have been named after my grandmother whom I never knew. They had moved to Hillsdale County from a town in Ohio and never fully accepted the hard life of pioneers. When a settlement began to form near them, they moved and set up a general store there. They kept the farm for a while, at least until my father, Mathew Jr., finished school and went into the military.

My grandfather's family had settled in...

I scanned ahead, for I was not especially interested in the confusing family tree information that followed. I noted that there was a mixture of farmers, tradesmen, and merchants in their family. That would be good background to help understand the various career choices that Colonel Benning seemed to pursue in his lifetime, but I skipped down a couple of paragraphs.

My father had entered the military in 1857 and enrolled in officer's school, planning to make it a career. He had studied surveying and building, which were skills sought after by the army. He enjoyed the army and advanced quickly.

I did not get much information about my father's military career from him. He was never very willing to share much information. I do remember once, when I was in high school, I was doing a paper about the Civil War times. The paper was more about President Lincoln's life than the war. I recall asking my father if he'd ever met him. My father became very stiff. He looked at the picture of Lincoln in my history book—sort of stared at it for a moment—and I distinctly remember what he said, and I quote: "He was a great man. He was my commander." And he struggled to lift his injured arm, and he saluted. Even at that young age,

I knew he had a reverent regard for President Lincoln and what he stood for.

I had to learn about my father's war record from researching other documents. I did get a copy of John Robertson's book Michigan in the War that was published in 1882. In it he tells of all the Michigan units. His book told me more than I could understand, but I was able to sketch out the following list of some details of his service and some of the battles he participated in:

1.  He was an officer in the Michigan 7th Cavalry organized in Grand Rapids in 1861.

2.  Being an officer, he participated in different assignments but stayed with the famed Michigan Brigade until discharge.

3.  He was a part of the battle of Shiloh, April of 1862; Battle of Angleton, Maryland, later in 1862; Gettysburg, Pennsylvania, in July of 1863; Frankton, Tennessee, early in 1864; and finally, the Battle of the Wilderness in May of 1864.

His battle record stopped there, and I found a confusing entry in one other resource that stated,

"Col. Matthew Benning died May 7, 1864, in the last stages of the Battle of the Wilderness. The body was never recognized and recovered. It is presumed he was interred in the mass graves of perished soldiers at the battlefield."

However, I had seen his discharge paper among his things, and he had obviously survived to become my father. He was discharged in January of 1865. This was before the war ended, so my confusion persisted. I did not get any clearer information for many years, and I will return to this later in my writing.

My father left the army and moved to the woods of Northern Michigan. He said one time he chose the spot on the hill where our farm was because it was clear with no woods around. I would find out more of his fear of the woods later.

My family was a small one…

I scanned down again, through the parts where Mrs. Anderson talked about her childhood, her siblings, and the dark mystery of her father's war career. I moved down quickly, reading only title sentences, a skimming technique I'd learned at the university. I stopped on one paragraph when I saw the oval symbol with *BFG* in the center; here she talked of his freight business and setting up of the store in Clam.

The next several paragraphs were about shipping, the store, and the young manager by the name of Anderson whom her father hired. "And the rest is history" I expected her to write, but she didn't.

Scanning again for several pages, a name stopped me short. She wrote, "His name is Jonas. He saved my life during the war." I quickly backed up a paragraph and began to read again.

I can only remember two other incidents when I was young when my father referred to the war. You see, my father was older when I was born, so he died before I was old or wise enough to seek more specific information from him.

In his aging years, his injured arm became more and more of a problem. It must have ached, and I remember my mother

rubbing salve on it and applying hot compresses. He would
sit in his favorite overstuffed chair by the fire with his arm
propped up on the arm. That is where I would sometimes sit
while he read to me when I was younger.

One day while he was sitting and my mother was applying compresses, there was a knock at the door. My mother asked me to
go and answer it. I must have been in my teens by then and reluctantly obeyed. I was shocked when I got to the door and was face-
to-face with the first Negro man I had ever seen. I gasped, and
my mother came to my side. She took my arm, leading me away,
and said gently over her shoulder, "I'll fetch Mathew."

I remember being rattled and couldn't figure out my mother's seeming calmness. My father rose with some difficulty,
holding his arm, and went to the door as my mother pulled
me off to the kitchen. She didn't berate me but hushed me
from saying anything as we both heard quiet voices from
the front of the house. My mother went on with her work,
and my curiosity led me to peek at the two men at the
door. My father had gone out on the porch with the man
by then, so I had to get closer to try to hear or possibly see
something.

My father may have sensed I was present, or he may have
just opened the door to grab his hat. But when he did, he
saw me and said, "Come here Bella. I want you to meet
someone." I followed, and I distinctly remember my father's
words: "This is Jonas. He saved my life during the war."
Again, my mother came and hurriedly took me back to work
with her in the kitchen. I wondered for years, but never heard
again anything more about that incident or my father's connections to this man.

Some years after my father died, I did have a chance to talk with my mother. I questioned her, and she curtly said, "Your father never talked about it, and he didn't want anybody to know anything about the war." After some coaxing, she relinquished this much information. Please be patient, for some of this information may be out of order due to how I heard the story; she recalled it in bits and pieces. My father entered the military with the intention of beginning a career and becoming an officer, several years before the Civil War. During the war, as an officer, he was in several units with several different jobs. Thus, he was in several awful battles.

The last battle was the Battle of the Wilderness. It was an awful affair in which the big guns were fairly useless because of the trees, which they ignited along with the forest brush. So the battle was made worse because the smoke and fire made it hard for the units to organize and keep track of one another. Many men were lost due to being overcome with the smoke; the wounded could not be retrieved; many bodies were burned.

My father, as an officer, was trying to save his troops when his horse was spooked, possibly by the flames or possibly because it was shot. My father was thrown from his horse and apparently hit his head, and that is all he remembered of the day.

My mother was very hesitant to tell more of the story. So I asked her bluntly, remembering my father's words those many years ago about the Negro man, "Who was Jonas, then? And why did Father say he had saved his life? And why did I find one source that claimed Father had been killed in the battle and his body never recovered?"

My mother was sitting in that same overstuffed chair I spoke of as being my father's favorite chair. She was probably knitting, as she often did. Maybe my father's spirit was still at that chair and gave her courage to proceed. But she looked at me awhile before sharing the following:

Your father woke in a bed somewhere but could not see, for there were bandages over his face and his arms. He was apparently feverish and in awful pain and went in and out of consciousness, we were told. He said he remembered only waking for short times and hearing a soft voice. The voice was always encouraging him to drink or eat some food. This went on for some time, maybe as long as a month. As he began to gain more consciousness, he determined he must be in an army hospital somewhere. Mostly he only heard the one voice urging him to drink, eat, and move. He claimed the first word he finally said—for remember he was badly burned and the smoke must have scorched his vocal cords—was 'hospital,' and the only answer he said he got was a short 'no' from the same soft voice.

As he got stronger, he could hear more and sensed there were two voices. Along with the soft voice, presumably a woman's, he heard a man's voice. The first time he remembered hearing the man was when he said, "Here. We will help you sit up, and we will remove the bandages." Most of this time, he was bandaged, or the bandages would be removed a little at a time and a salve applied to his wounds. He remembered it stunk badly. The first time they removed the bandages, he still could not see anything but light.

After that they took them off more often and would leave them off for some time before replacing them. One day after several months, when the bandages came off, he could see figures and movement. Everyone was excited, and as his sight returned, he was most surprised. He found out that his care-takers were a Negro couple and he was in their home. He had not heard any fighting, so he presumed they were a long way from the battlefield, but he had no idea where or how far.

He stayed with them, and they helped him recover. You remember, his arm was always bad, for it had been broken and this couple had no way to take care of it properly, so it had remained how it was. The more serious wounds were his burns, as we could all tell. However, I cannot imagine how they treated those burns for so long and with so much success to keep them from scarring.

Anyway, your father was a loyal military man and insisted that as soon as his health returned he would return to his unit. The host—"

I interrupted my mother and said, "The host must have been the man, Jonas."

Yes, you are right. Jonas had explained to your father that he was fighting near their unit in the forest and had seen your father fall. He had been 'recruited' or ordered to join another Union unit to help scout for them because he was local and knew the area. He had been fighting with that group for over a week when they got to the wilderness. So he dragged your father out of the fighting, and who knows how they got back to Jonas's home where they cared for him."

My mother rubbed her temples as she struggled to remember details.

Where was I now? Oh, yes, he wanted to return to his army
unit. They argued some, but Jonas agreed to help him back
to the Union lines. Your father did not know where he was;
he and Jonas walked for a long time. They had to go mostly
by night to miss the rebel units in the area, but they finally
arrived at a Union camp. Your father was planning to have
Jonas stay there where it was safer, but he basically turned
around, and Jonas was gone. Because of your father's injuries,
they cleared up his record and discharged him, and he came to
this area."

My mother's story had always touched me; I had always
wanted to write a book about their lives, and this is the closest
I have come.

I stopped and reread her mother's remembrances before skimming on. Mrs. Anderson filled in the rest of her family's story of
growing up at the store in Clam River after she married the manager, Mr. Anderson.

I just sat for some time thinking about all that I had read. I
instantly had a dozen questions I wished I could ask Mrs. Anderson
about missing information. This was amazing, and I leafed back
in the pages and reread parts I'd read before. My mind was flying
trying to connect this information with what else I had discovered,
but all the thinking and wondering always came back to the same
questions: could Colonel Benning's friend Jonas and the Jonas I had
met be related, and what's more, could they all be a part of the
same story?

I put the materials away and walked outside. There was no moon and little sound, and the wind blew up from the lake that night. Yes, I heard it clearly: the loon's voice seemed to clear the air and say all was well. It was well, and I was ready for another day. I was ready to work to find more answers. I smiled and went inside to bed.

# 21 - Jackson's Bible

*When Jonas came up from the South,*

*He came with unlikely help*

*From a friend who had regained his health.*

*Dangers and intrigue abound.*

*The rail trip it was daring.*

*Passengers hid so as not to be found.*

*How could all this be?*

*As we are uncovering for all to see,*

*That history's alive, buzzing as a bee.*

*It's all right here, right where I am*

*On the lake, by the store, by the River Clam.*

The beginning of the week was busy. I noticed Millie's station wagon come and go at Jack's. I thought they were only coming for the weekend, but it looked like she was staying for a longer visit. There was a rack on the car for a canoe or a rowboat. I knew there were some grandchildren by the suits I had seen at my last visit.

Part of that mystery was solved later in the week. I was at the checkout counter in the store; there was a steady stream of customers, so I didn't notice the young man standing to the right of the door by the newspaper rack. It was not unusual for folk to stop to peruse the paper or a magazine. Most went ahead and bought something so it wasn't a problem like loitering or anything; this young man just stood there, though, and I finally noticed he didn't seem to be looking at or for anything.

I got a break at the checkout, so I asked if I could help him find anything. He shyly came over to my counter.

"Are you Ron?" he asked.

I smiled and acknowledged I was indeed that person.

He looked down and hesitated before he said, "My grandpa sent me over here with this note."

He dug in his rumpled shorts and produced a thrice-folded square of paper and pushed it to me on the counter.

I was a bit surprised and asked him, "Are you Millie's son?" I got a nod of recognition. "Are you staying for some vacation?"

"Just a couple more days," he stated matter-of-factly.

I had a customer coming to the checkout, but I wasn't sure if this was a crisis and whether or not I was needed. So I stuttered out a question.

"Is your grandpa OK?" I may have sounded a bit desperate.

"Oh, yeah! He is as cranky as ever!" We locked eyes, and as we laughed together, his eyes seemed to twinkle like Jack's. I guess this kid had inherited his grandpa's humor as well.

"Well, thanks, and tell Jack and your mom I said 'Hi'. I've got to get back to work; tell them I'll see them later."

He waved as he went out the door. I pushed the note into my pocket and directed my attention back to the customer standing next in line.

Several hours later I was on my break, and I felt for the paper in my pocket. As I sat at the picnic table by the store's back door, I opened it. I was pleased to find it was a poem. I began to read:

Oh, woe am I!
For it is for quiet that I yearn.
I love my children all,
But I wish they'd learn
To come for shorter visits
And not linger here
For I cannot rest
Or even snitch a beer!
The kids are here.
They talk and yell
Yet when they speak
Don't know what they say or what they tell.


She's hidden my pipe,
Makes me eat every meal.
I can't think for myself.

Mother Hen thinks it's all a big deal!
The cat is the smart one.
He's run off and hid;
Otherwise this chaos would
Cause him to blow his lid.
Two days more, or so everyone says,
Looking forward to quiet and sleeping late.
Hope you are well, and don't worry!
I'll survive this cruel fate! !   (It was signed: Jack and the cat)
I laughed out loud and read it again. I must have been giggling, for Dave came outside.

"What in heaven's name is so funny?"

I just laughed and handed him the paper as I finished my soft drink. He read it, smiled, and with a chuckle, said, "Is this your friend Jack from over across the way? He is definitely a funny man! And he writes poetry! He fascinates me. Maybe you could introduce us sometime?"

"Sure, why not?"

I refolded the paper, and still chuckling a bit, Dave and I went back to work, for the place was very busy.

I left the river late that evening after Dave and I had stopped over to see Dan for a few minutes. The bar was sort of noisy and busy, so we didn't hang around. I slowed passing Jack's on my way home and was surprised to see lights still on. I smiled—as he'd said, he couldn't get any rest. They seemed to have a bonfire built toward the beach. I smiled hoping they weren't burning up all the *BFG* boards, and my mind switched to focusing on my visit tomorrow with Jonas and his wife.

Jonas and his wife were sitting outside when I arrived in the early evening. They were sitting in some chairs along the stones where the flowers were planted. They both smiled, and the missus waved as I got out of the car.

"It's a beautiful evening for sitting!" I said as I approached. Jonas got up stiffly and folded his chair. He moved and leaned it against the house by the door. The missus had some knitting or maybe darning in her lap. She gathered the yarn and stuck the needle into the roll just like I'd seen my mother do numerous times.

"You's come on inside." she said as she, too, rose stiffly.

"I'm always honored to be your guest." As I said that, she looked at me, smiled, and gave a motherly wave of her hand.

"Oh, you's is always so sweet!"

Jonas proceeded to pick up her chair, fold it up, and put it with the other. He joined us as we all went into the house. So far he had not said a word, and I wondered if he was upset or bothered in some way. When he did speak, I was looking and listening for clues, but he only said, "Come on in and sit, son."

Mrs. Jackson set three glasses on the table and got a pitcher from the refrigerator.

"Iced tea?"

Jonas and I both nodded. He took his glass and sipped some. We sat quietly for a moment, and my nervousness must have bubbled over, as I said, "I don't know where to start with questions."

Jonas reached over and, putting his hand on my arm, said softly to his wife, "Mama, bring us da Bible."

I was a bit confused. She went into the other room and returned with a large book. She laid it on the center of the table. I could see then that it was one of those rather ornately covered Bibles. Jonas opened it to the very middle, and I noticed there were numerous papers there. Several of the papers fell out, and Mrs. Jackson gathered them together.

I remember that my grandfather had a Bible similar to this one and how in the very middle there were some pages that included family information. Often families used to keep what some called a "family tree" of names and dates there. My grandfather referred to our Bible as the "family Bible," I suppose because of all the family information included in it. I noticed that Jonas's Bible had a chart like list of a similar kind. Mrs. Jackson pulled out a photograph from the pages and showed it to me.

"This here's ma daddy whose name was also Jonas."

I could see he was a large, rugged man, and he also looked fairly tall. The picture appeared to have been taken of him in his older years, as he had white hair and a white beard. He had deep black eyes and a firm but not grim expression on his face.

"He's was a slave as a young man, as was his daddy and probably his daddy before him. We's don't knows all our family history, but we's know that he and my momma lived on a farm in Virgini' somewhere. How's they got here is the story I think you's are a needin' to hear. Has you 's heard of what they's called the Underground Railroad?"

I nodded.

"My mammy and pap came here on that rail. Up this far north was not a popular route. Most peoples came on the rail and wents to Canada through Detroit. Comin' here is a bit of an odd story."

She paused and looked at Jonas. I glanced at both, trying to read the nonverbal communication going on between them. I couldn't get a clue and was surprised to hear Jonas speak next.

"You sees, my kin was slaves on da same farm, and Jonas there helped all of 'em get out of Virgini'."

Missus went on speaking to me. "What has you's found out about Colonel Benning?"

I retrieved my notes from my backpack under the chair and told of the oral history I had found. I noticed Mrs. Jackson's eyes begin to water when I shared that although assumed dead by the army, Colonel Benning was saved and nursed to health by a black couple.

The missus looked at me deeply, with tears in her eyes, tapped her finger on the picture, and said, "This here be da man done saved your colonel."

I was awestruck and only beginning to sense the puzzle pieces coming together. We just sat, and I could tell we were all struck by the coincidences that had brought us together. After a few minutes, I went on.

"Mrs. Anderson's name was Bella Benning; she was the colonel's daughter. She married Mr. Anderson, who ran the store in Clam

River, which I believe may have also been owned by Colonel Benning. Mrs. Anderson only recalled one incident before her father died when a black man came to their house and her father introduced him to her. He said, 'Bella, this is Jonas who saved my life during the war.'"

Mrs. Jackson cut in. "Again, young man, you's need to know how important it was for us coloreds to stay way far in the background. I guess my father done found work in a lumber camp that was isolated, and my momma cooked there. They's woulda never been welcome to live in town, not in any of these here towns 'round about." She swirled her hand around over her head to indicate the surrounding area.

"But why?" I looked for words, trying not to seem too dumb. "Why did Jonas and your family stay in this area and not go on to Canada or some other friendlier place?"

Again they exchanged glances, and I felt the electricity sparking between them.

"That there's another story we's needs to share, too, but I's want to go back to one thing we left out when talking about Colonel Benning."

As if on cue, Jonas reached down behind his chair and retrieved a short board. Before he laid it on the table, I just knew what it was. He turned it over to reveal the now-familiar BFG logo.

"Benning Freight Goods," I stated. Then, looking at Jonas, I added, "But you called it something else that day. But what?"

Jonas began to hum, and then he sang, "This train is bound for glory, this train."

"That's it! Hold it! Can you wait while I retrieve a book from my car? I was going to ask you something about it, and I forgot to bring it in."

I quickly left and was soon back in a breathless rush with Jack's book. I put it on the table, and they both leaned in to read the title: *The History of Cassopolis and Their Part in the Underground Railroad*.

Again they glanced knowingly at each other. The missus grinned at me and commented, "I be guessin' you's been doing your homework, son. I's impressed you's care enough to study some."

I explained how my friend Jack had lived on a farm in Cass County. "In his old age," I said, "ever since his wife died, he's lived with his daughter in Cassopolis. He explained she'd gotten him this book for Christmas; he brought it up to the cottage with him and lent it to me."

I quickly opened it to the table of contents and ran my finger down the list. Stopping on the one line I was looking for, I turned the book to them and read the title: "Chapter 11: 'Bound for Glory' and Other Songs."

They both smiled, and Jonas resumed his humming and singing of the chorus. The missus hushed him and said, "You see, son, smugglin' slaves out of da South was plenty dangerous. They's had codes and signs and things to lead them on the Railroad. They's had to be hidden and they's often traveled at night."

"By's da time Jonas, my father, comed north it was after da war. But even after the 'mancipation, many Southern folk would still search out and punish dere slaves for leavin'. The slaves had no power or authority and no protection or guns. Even the 'ol government wasn't strong enough to stop all them problems, and many were kept in da South, and you might as well a called 'em slaves."

Mrs. Jackson's voice was getting louder, and I could easily detect her passionate hatred of that slavery history. Jonas spoke up to add something or maybe just to calm her down.

"As you's said, Daddy Jonas done nursed the colonel back to health after them awful wounds in dat woods fight...I can't recall da name?"

"The Battle of the Wilderness," I said.

"Yes, sir dat's why he lived on that there hill in that open field away from da trees. Daddy Jonas told us da colonel was so petrified of dem woods, he never did come out's to da lumber camp where they's worked all dose years because of its being so deep in dawoods."

As he was talking, I saw Mrs. Jackson open to the chapter about the songs. She said, "You sees here, there was symbols and songs. 'Follow the Drinking Gourd' meant to follow the North Star and the Big Dipper—the 'Drinking Gourd.' The cup became one of the favorite symbols, and they'd draw it in da mud or carve it on's a tree.

"Lots dem songs made reference to trains or railroads. One of my mother's favorites went 'this gospel train's a-comin', comin' on down that track.' But now I can't remember the tune. Another song was 'Wade in the Water.' My mammy explained they'd often walk in da water of rivers and creeks so's da dogs couldn't follow they's scent. Also da rivers and creeks would lead them to bigger rivers and on to da Ohio or da Mississippi so's they'd get on north."

She paused and then started to sing softly, and her low, almost-base voice seemed to accentuate the moment and the song.

"Wade in the water. Wade in the water, children.

Wade in the water. God's gonna trouble the water."


No one spoke. It was a reverent moment. I was being given a great gift, a glimpse deep into the souls of my Negro friends. I felt myself getting teary at the awesomeness of the time. It was definitely like a church, as the missus had described the incident during the storm.

Jonas spoke and, pointing to the board, said, "Do you's see it now, son? 'BFG' was 'Benning Freight Goods' to da white folk, but to Daddy Jonas and ma peoples it was 'Bound For Glory,' following the rail out of that devil's invention called slavery." He hummed a bit, and then he sang softly and reverently,

"This train is bound for glory, this train.

This train is bound for glory, this train.

This train is bound for glory.

Don't carry nothing but the righteous and the holy.

This train is bound for glory, this train.

"Your colonel went back after his discharge and somehow found Jonas's family and convinced dem to come north. He planned it mighty thorough and set up da Benning Freight business, but his freight was Negro folk."

"Would he have smuggled them in the freight containers?"

Jonas and the missus nodded, and my face lit up!

"This is the same way they smuggled the booze later during Prohibition! They hid it in the regular freight boxes, opened them at night, and took out the booze. They'd reseal the boxes and send them on to their planned shipping destination. These were smuggling jobs done for two different purposes, several decades apart!"

They both smiled in obvious agreement. The missus shuffled the papers again. She pulled out a yellowed sheet. As she turned it to me, I determined it was an invoice of some kind. She slid it across the table closer to me. At the top it said *Benning Freight Goods*. The date was smudged and unreadable except for the year. I made it out to be *1866*.

"Just after the war," I muttered to myself, but I realized I must have said it loudly enough for them to hear.

"Look here," said the missus, pointing to the lines indicating the contents. I read:

>     2 F's — FMCC
>            — MC
>     3 M
>     2 F
>     3 C

"What you's think that means?" She looked at me knowingly, with a glint in her eye.

In recognition and awe, I nearly whispered, "Two families, one with a father, a mother, and two children and the second with just a mother and child; three single men; two single women; and three unattached children."

She settled back in her chair and sipped her tea. She smiled slyly and gave out a satisfied sigh. I was speechless.

Finally my mind began to wrap around all this, but there was still the unanswered question of "why here?" You said earlier that most went on to Canada. Why did your family stay here?"

"Yes, son, most folk hads to go on to Canada, 'specially before the war. Then there was a law dat police people could come up here and drags you back to slavery."

"Unbelievable," I said.

"Yes, very unbelievable sure. Even though Daddy Jonas's family and da Jacksons here came after the war, theys did not feel safe and figured to go on across the state and get a steamer to Canada."

"Something serious must have stopped them. Is that what you're saying?"

Those glances went back and forth again. The Mrs. Jackson spoke, slowly at first.

"Yes, there was a awful accident one night at your very Clam River. Ma mammy and pap had come on an earlier shipment." She paused and tapped the BFG board. "They were waiting for the others hidden someplace by the river."

"The tunnel!" I blurted out. "That is what the tunnel was for. It wasn't built to smuggle booze but to smuggle slaves. It was only handy for the booze some decades later. I bet the tunnel goes from that boathouse in the woods to the cabin and was built before the river changed its course."

They both got puzzled looks on their faces and just stared at me.

"Oh, I'll take you there soon and show you. This all fits, and Jack will love to meet you and share in your story. But that will be for later. Excuse me, ma'am, for I interrupted your story."

They gathered themselves again and went on. The missus spoke.

"Included in that there second shipment was my aunt, that be my mother's sister, and her husband. They's had three children with dem. One of dem was a small baby who was only one month old. Da way my mammy told da story, there's was a bad storm that night when their boat arrived. Those waitin' couldn't go's outside and help for it was plumb too dangerous they's be discovered. So's as them passengers tried to land and git off'n da boat themselves, my aunt was thrown down, and da baby fell into the water."

I gasped; my heart was racing.

"Yes, you's imagine the worst, and you's be correct. Dat baby done fell into the dark water and drowned."

She paused again to gather her composure. She took a hankie out from her apron pocket and daubed her tears before going on.

"My auntie was mightily distraught. She screamed and screamed. The others were afraid she'd give away their presence, so apparently my father hit her and knocked her out. Sometime later, in the night, they were prepared to leave by a wagon. But my auntie woke again and began to scream uncontrollably. They had to silence her for fear of discovery. I do not know if my pap had to hit her again, but it just sounds awful."

She hung her head and began to sob. Jonas immediately reached over, patting her arm to comfort her. Soon she composed herself.

"But—" I began. The missus held up her hand to hush me and continued.

"Late dat night, somewhere on the trail, my distraught aunt woke, screamed, and while madly beatin' whoever was with her, jumped off'n that there wagon and ran away. Her last words while runnin' into the woods were 'I's not a lea'ein' my baby!'"

Jonas added, "You see, theys had hurriedly buried the baby. Maybe in that there tunnel you spoke of or near by. Theys had to be secretive and move quickly."

"So..." Taking a deep breath and exhaling slowly, the missus came to the end of her story. "My mother begged Daddy Jonas not's to leave her sister. They's got off dat wagon and made da others go on without them. Dat simply's why ma parents ended up stayin' here."

Jonas added his own ending. "My kin went on to da last station on da east side of the state. Some caught the steamer to Canada, but for some reason I was never told they's stayed there. My father was able to gets hisself a job in the huge quarry there, and later on my siblings and I were born. Therefore, I's grew up in a small burg outside of Alpena. I heard o' the missus here through other kin, and so…" He leaned over, took her hand again, and smiled. "And so here's we are."

This adventurous, tragic, and courageous story had left me hardly breathing. I could barely begin to comprehend the danger and fear they still held within them. I got a glimpse of their reluctance and fear to talk to me even this many years later.

We had to end our time together. The missus began to pick up the paper, and a newspaper clipping fell out from the stack. The headline grabbed my attention, and I put my hand on it as she was trying to retrieve it. The headline read "The Howler Legend," and we all looked at it and one another questioningly.

"We are not done with this story yet!" I said as we all stood there frozen.

❧

# 22 - The Legend

When the sounds they howl,
Everyone has a theory;
Everyone has a clue.
In the end they missed it by a mile.
The Clam River rats are a hardy lot,
So it's no surprise to find a plot
Along the river wharfs, left to rot.
The mystery runs deep and cold
On the shores of the River Clam.

A lantern's flash and a dark boat near.
Midnight visitors seem mighty queer.
Dark figures come on and off,
But the storm was at hand,
And the boat it was lashed,
Shaken, and tossed; a small body splashed
In the dark, and no one could retrieve
The small baby lost. Left the mother to grieve.
Distraught was not a word to describe
This mother's anguish there,
But silence was the code.
Her screams reached the highest air.
She was muffled for fear of uncovering the plan.
For the mystery runs deep and cold
On the shores of the River Clam.

The next day, I made copies of the article Mrs. Jackson had shared. The clipping was from a local paper, she recalled, and was probably ten or more years old. However, it had no dates on it or even an author or reporter byline, so I was really at a loss as to how to do any tracing. "Maybe I will ask the helpful librarian," I thought. "She may recall its origin." The article read as follows:

All places have stories. In our area there are stories about logging adventures, the first settlers, and old Native American camping grounds; the list goes on. Because of the many lakes, there are numerous tales of huge fish being caught or almost caught. There are legends of events surrounding almost any normal part of the life lived in this particular area.

We all know of some other famous places and their legends. The first to come to mind would be the quiet Loch Ness with its famous serpentine monster. There are many Bigfoot or Yeti sightings, too. Spooky places, "hauntings," and UFOs all fall into that category of the seemingly endless list of local legends.

Have you ever heard a strange sound? Maybe you have heard something from your basement or attic or old barn out back? We have our own local legend that revolves around strange sounds. Like with most legends, all of the "reporters" seem to hear such a wide variety of things that truth is obscured and very hard to locate. As in our local case, the sound seems to come from the hilly country where there are long, echoing valleys and the wide-open waters of the many popular lakes.

A sound can only be described by comparing it to another. For instance, a sound could be described as a "cry like a baby's" or a "bark like a dog's." Comparison adds difficulty because what sounds like a "woman's scream" to one person may sound like the "squeak of an old door hinge" to another.

I am referring to our local legend that, in a couple references I found, is referred to as the "Howling Hills" mystery. The reports all seem to agree that it involves the hearing of a "strange sound." It has variously been described as a "howl like a wolf's" or a "yipping howl like a coyote's." Some report it as more like a moaning, groaning, crying, or sobbing sound. Most have agreed the sound lasts for a time of several minutes. Here another oddity is that even though the sound lasts for some minutes in an area, it is sometimes not heard again there for several years. The intermittency adds another element of difficulty to locating and/or identifying the sound.

There are many skeptics. I had several tell me, "I've heard of that old tale, and I don't believe it at all. I think someone is doing too much drinking, most likely." There are lots of skeptics and lots of explanations for why this is not true. But there are no skeptics among people who have heard this unexplainable something.

The article was an interesting read, but it did nothing to identify or locate any specifics about this sound. I knew I had heard something, so I was certainly not one of the skeptics. Jack was with me on this one, but why was the article in Jonas's bible? I decided to write to them, for

I couldn't see a time to get over there again soon, and I wanted to convince them to come to meet Jack. So I wrote them this letter:

Dear Jonas and Mrs. Jackson,

I am anxious for us to gather again soon and for you to meet my friend Jack. I am sure he will be glad to meet you. I can pick you up on Monday, and we'll return in a few short hours. Please come with me. I believe it will help us all fill in pieces of the story we are all a part of now.

One question for you to explain is why the article about the Howling Hills Mystery was kept in your Bible. Did your mother share that article? The main idea that has rattled in my brain is that it might be connected with your aunt living off in the woods. Was she a crazy woman who continued to grieve? Did your mother have contact with her?

You need to know that Jack and I have both, on more than one occasion, heard a strange sound at the cabin. Jack reports that in his twenty-five years of coming to the cabin, he has heard it several dozen times. He says it is mostly a low moaning or groaning sound. I know a visit there will help us all.

Lastly, I had an unusual experience about six years ago. I had simply put it out of my mind until now. With all this new learning I'm doing, I think I can share this event.

As you know we live on a farm in the very hills up off the lake where the sounds have been reported. As I grew up, I worked there for my father. He always had a variety of folk working for him. I remember one time, soon after moving here, I was working with an older man, Harold, who often came to the farm to pick fruit or do other work. It was hard for me as a young teen to feel comfortable around Harold, for he did not speak or hear.

I hated the phrase "deaf and dumb," for he was certainly smart; it was just that he could not communicate easily. He spoke using many gestures and kind of grunts. He did not have very many teeth, either, which didn't help. It was scary at first, but we became fast friends. He was poor and lived sometimes in one of my father's old tenant houses down the road. He did have an unfortunate habit of using too much alcohol. I do recall my father retrieving him from the local bar when he was needed for work.

Anyway, one day Harold and I were to go down past the farm to gather something, maybe wood. I don't recall exactly except that we had the tractor and pulled a trailer. I was always interested in going down that two-track road because there were a couple of old homestead shacks in the woods. I liked to explore them; I was a curious kid. When my dad still had a riding horse, I'd come down this way, especially with my neighbor friend. She also had a horse, and we rode together occasionally.

Getting back to the story, we were driving along, and I stopped near one of those old shacks. I got off the tractor, and Harold got quite agitated. I motioned with universal sign language that I needed to go and relieve myself. I went nearer the shack, and Harold got off the wagon quickly. He was old— over seventy, I think—and I was surprised to see him move that fast. He hurried over to me and grabbed my shoulder, shaking his head and pointing to the shack.

I smiled and shrugged it off, but he was very agitated. I became troubled but obliged and returned to the tractor and trailer. When we got back, Harold pulled the ever-present pad of paper from his pocket and retrieved his stub of a pencil from another pocket in his bib overalls.

He motioned for me to follow and read as he wrote "HAG HOUSE" on the pad. I put my hands up to indicate I didn't understand. He then motioned, pointing to himself and putting his hand down low. I could tell he meant to say something having to do with when he was very small or very young.

He then signed walking and holding the hand of a taller person. I presumed he meant he had come here as a child with some adult, maybe his mother. He put his hands to his head and faked crying, presumably to indicate that it was a very scary time. He seemed frustrated and unable to communicate more with signs, so he again got out his pad. He wrote, "HAG HERBS."

I thought for a moment and then reached down and pulled up some weeds. He nodded yes, pulled some more, and rubbed them on his arm. Then he rubbed his stomach like he was sick. He signed stirring in a cup and drinking and then rubbed his stomach and smiled as if it were all OK. I talked with my mother after we returned home, and she confirmed that his family had probably made teas and medicines from the herbs. It was very common among rural people.

I smiled and nodded in recognition and turned to finish my goal. Harold quickly grabbed my shoulder a second time;

he was still agitated. He pointed to the shack and shook his head. He then made a scary figure with his arms arched toward me, as if to indicate a monster. Then without words he put his hands to his mouth and made a sound, sort of like a...I can't really describe it, but now I would use the word "howl."

I came back to the wagon, and he wrote, "HAG HERBS HOWL." It made no sense back then, but now I think it may be fitting into this story. I assumed there must have been an old woman who lived there when he was a young child. His mother had brought him there, and it had scared him greatly. They must have bought or traded for herbs, but the howl thing never fit until now.

The "Howling Hills Mystery" must be connected to your family's history. Your aunt must surely be dead now, yet the sounds continue. I do not know much about the spirit world, but please come with me to Jack's. I think it will help us all. I will see you Monday.

Blessings to you both,

Ron


There was one other unusual related piece I retrieved from my mother's things. Actually, when I told her about some of the story, she went and got the newspaper clipping. It was a short article from our local paper from just a couple years back, and it referred to the howling and connected it to my father and his use of a certain fruit-farming tool. It read as follows:

Headline: *Howling Hills Mystery Solved at Bellaire*

Bellaire – The case of the "Howling Hills of Bellaire" has
finally been solved, after creating several hair-raising midnight sensations for local residents. The eerie sound of a siren
at half-pitch echoing among the hills above the town accompa-
nied by northern lights and the howling of dogs—all during
the usually quiet hours of midnight—had everyone mystified.

Someone noticed that the sound occurred after rain when the
air was cool and there was no wind blowing. Further investiga-
tion revealed that the source was a ridge that is the west bor-
der of the Intermediate River valley and that there are several
cherry and apple orchards on the ridge.

The siren like noise was made by a large machine used for
dusting the fruit trees. The owner of Hilltop Orchards
explains that the dusting must be done as soon as possible after
rain, thus necessitating frequent night work.

The noise of the duster spread down the valley and was magnified by the stillness of the night. Dogs, especially sensitive
to sirens, howled, and northern lights, which usually show on
calm, cool nights, provided an appropriate backdrop.

Again I had no author or reporter to follow-up with and interview. There was no date on this, although a careful search of some
newspaper archives could have been fruitful. I had no time for that,

but I did make several copies so I could share it with the Jacksons and with Jack. I would have hated to tell that reporter how what he or she found out was only the tip of the iceberg. I didn't think the headline was correct, for the "Howling Hills Mystery" had *NOT* been solved. But it may be soon.

# 23 - Bound for Glory

*When the story's told,*

*No matter how young or how old,*

*The mystery deepens, and the love*

*Gets thick between an unlikely trove*

*Of old and sage, young and little age.*

*A dark heart full of love will always win.*

*An open door or heart will welcome you in.*

It was hard to convince them to come. I went to see them later in the week and I could tell Jonas was hesitant to come see Jack. Mrs. Jackson showed me my letter had arrived. "This here's very close to what I's remember as a child."

"That is exactly why I need you to come with me." Mrs. Jackson looked hard at Jonas as I coaxed and cajoled until Jonas agreed to join me and visit Jack. I picked them up in the afternoon that Monday the following week and drove to Clam River. It appeared it had been a long time since they had ventured out in this direction, if they ever had. I began to wonder how that mistrust and fear had fostered the isolation of living "in the shadows," as the missus had put it.

I drove into Jack's drive and was glad to see him waiting for us. I had never seen Jack look so charming. He was the perfect host, welcoming and inviting; I noticed he'd gone all out and brought his small table out on the porch and that glasses and a pitcher were placed on it. I was impressed.

"Jack, this is Jonas Jackson and his lovely wife. Jonas, this is Jack."

Jack's smile and their similar age both seemed to do much to put them at ease, and a smile actually appeared on Jonas's usually sober face. They shook hands easily and cordially. The missus stepped forward and introduced herself, and I was shocked, not at her boldness but because I realized I'd never heard her first name before now.

"I am Pearl Jackson, and I's pleased to meet you, Mr. Jack. We's become plenty fond of yoo' young friend here."

I blushed as she pulled on my arm. I was shocked again because I'd never thought of her as affectionate. But I liked hearing her name—Pearl—and I let it roll off my mind's tongue. It sounds good—Jonas and Pearl—and I smiled to myself.

"Come up here and sit," Jack cordially directed. "But watch your step."

We all moved slowly onto the porch. I could see Jonas was silently surveying the area. Mrs. Jackson spoke first.

"Thank you for invitin' us to yoo home. Da flowers are beautiful."

"Thank you, ma'am. Ron here tells me you enjoy flowers, too. My late wife was very fond of pansies, and I keep them sort of for her." Jack got a sad expression on his face.

Missus reached out and touched his arm. "I'm so sorry for your loss. I's knowed you two was a blessin' to each other."

Jack smiled with a softness I don't recall I'd ever seen or at least noticed before. It felt warm and good.

Jonas had taken a few steps toward the lake. "You's got a mighty beautiful view here, Mr. Jack."

Jack brightened again, moved toward Jonas, and agreed.

"Yes, and good sunsets, too. Grandkids sure enjoyed it this week; they had a boat and all. It was good to see it busy and used, but they about wore me out!" They both chuckled.

"Me and the missus was never blessed with chillin'. But we's got a mess of nieces and nephews."

"Please sit." Jack motioned us all to the table. His two chairs from inside were there, and he directed Pearl and Jonas to sit in them.

"Pull up those two foldin' chairs there," he said to me. I grabbed them and opened them for Jack and me.

"About all I've got is iced tea and water. Oh, yes, I have one can of cola left. Those kids about cleaned me out!"

Jonas replied, "Iced tea is fine, sir."

"But with sugar, correct, Mr. Jonas?" I chimed in with a grin.

He nodded, and Jack asked me, "Son, would you go grab the sugar bowl off the counter by the sink and bring a couple spoons, too?"

I opened the screen, and out scooted Jack the cat to inspect what was going on. As cats do, he went immediately to Jonas and the missus with no inhibitions.

"Oh!" Mrs. Jackson sort of jumped in surprise but smiled, reached down, and petted Jack. "Oh, a kitty!"

Jack spoke up. "Oh, get away, you old fool. Don't bother these nice folk."

"No bother," Pearl responded. Her touch had already set off Jack's patented loud purr. "He's a obviously enjoyin' it!"

"I see he returned," I said to Jack.

He looked at me closely and replied, "So, I see you got my note, eh? Heck, he was back here within minutes of that car leavin'. Strange animal, that cat!"

"We's haven't had a cat in some years," Jonas piped up. "Strays just shows up once in a while, and I's encourage them so's to keep control of the mice."

As usual Jack (the cat) only needed a small bit of recognition, and he rambled off down the steps in search of who knows what.

Jack (the man) offered the guests a small plate of goodies. "Sorry I'm a bit shy of offerings. Those kids, you know! But help yourself, please. There are still a couple of goodies, and that's a piece of banana bread my daughter baked."

"Thank you for your kindness," Pearl said and then sampled the banana bread.

Jonas cleared his throat and began, "So, Ron here done brought us a packin' crate board with dat BFG logo on it. We's was both shocked, for we's never known of any other connections."

"Yes, can you share that connection?" Jack said.

I stepped into the conversation at this point. I got out the notes and began to fill Jack in on what the Jacksons and I had shared in our last conversation. First, I explained about Colonel Benning's war record and his moving to this area. "He had been rescued in the battle by Pearl's father when the latter was a very young slave on a farm in Virginia. Colonel Benning then proceeded to develop the elaborate plan to rescue them and bring them to safety in the North. The freight company was a cover for the smuggling of slaves just like it later became a cover for the smuggling of the booze during Prohibition."

Jack interrupted and filled Jonas and Pearl in on his own story. "My father came here from Cass County to marry one of the Anderson girls from the store over yonder." He motioned to the store. "That's the same store Ron here works at now. My mother had died, and I had a job in Cass, so I didn't come up here very often. On one of those visits, my father told of his exploits during Prohibition, and the tunnel…" Jack stopped and looked at me.

"We'll get to that in a second, but let me continue to fill in some of the blanks in the story." I went on in collecting all the details of this amazing puzzle. I talked faster as I got more excited.

At a pause, we all took a breath and sipped our tea. Jack spoke up.

"Ron has found out that the river was changed a long time ago, about 1875. It used to run near the front of this cottage, sort of where your car is parked. It must have been that way when your families arrived here, and the tunnel..." Jack stopped quickly and looked at all of us; a kind of recognition came over him. "And the tunnel does not go to the bar because that would be the wrong direction. Actually, I'll bet it goes to that old boathouse out there! Don't you guess?" he said to me. "And it must have caved in after they changed the course of the river and then put the road in over it like it is now!"

Jonas and Pearl looked confused as I smiled and nodded agreement to Jack.

"Could we'all see the tunnel?" Jonas spoke with a noticeable crack in his voice. He reached over tenderly and rested his hand on Pearl's arm. They were both noticeably emotional. If these connections were true, we were touching a deep core in the history of their lives. I again got that feeling of awe in my gut.

"Ron, here is the key. You all be very careful; it's not a very good set of steps. I'll grab my big light."

With that, Jack stepped inside and emerged with the flashlight in hand. I helped Mrs. Jackson and Jonas back off the porch, and we all moved to the rear of the house. I unlocked the door and opened it wide.

"Kind of musty place, I'm afraid," Jack apologized. "You go first, kid, and clear out the cobwebs."

They all smiled, and I went forth with the light. My eyes adjusted to the darkness soon enough, and I turned to be sure Jonas would not stumble. He and Jack descended, and I heard Pearl say, "No, thank you, just now. I'll wait here for you'all."

As we moved across the space, as I'd done with Jack before, I motioned to the box with the BFG brand, and Jonas nodded his recognition. We came to the hidden door. Jack reached for the latch-string and pulled the door open. Jonas gasped and grabbed my arm.

"Oh my God, there be a door near identical to this here on one of my's outbuildin's! Maybe the same...maybe da same folk built it out of those there packin' crate boards?"

I could feel his emotions rising and put my hand on his arm; I hoped he wouldn't think I was acting too familiar.

Jack took the light now and shown it into the small space and explained.

"It has always been like this since I first saw it back in the thirties, but if you look higher, you can tell it used to go back a long way. It has likely caved in due to being dug into this sand."

I spoke up. "Now I see what you mean, Jack! Paying more attention to the direction, it doesn't go to the bar, for it would have had to go under the river! It goes south, and I bet it goes to that old boathouse. However, with the river redirected and the road over top of it, it collapsed."

Everyone nodded in agreement, and then Jonas coughed.

"Let's go up top out of this mustiness," I heard Jack say as we turned and went carefully up the steps to where Pearl stood. We immediately saw the tears on her cheeks as she clutched her hankie and sobbed quietly.

Jonas went directly to her. "Are you's OK, dear?" He held her as she sobbed for a few moments.

"Jonas," she said, pulling away slightly and looking at him. "I's can feel der spirit here. I can! I can! Oh, Lord, I's can feel they's here with us! I's didn't feel it at first, but after you'all went down there, I heard a squeak and a moan…"

"We opened the tunnel door!" Jack said.

"It was like a cool breeze. I's felt the soft, gentle touch of der spirits. Oh, Lord, I's so blessed to has come here!"

As I closed and relocked the door, Jack beckoned, "Come, let's return to the porch out of this hot sun." We settled back in our chairs, and I refreshed the tea.

I spoke up. "Let me fill in a bit of the story if I can?" I looked at Pearl, who was wiping her eyes, and sought her permission; she nodded.

"The story Pearl shared was that her father, Jonas, was the slave who, with his young wife, nursed the colonel back to health after his terrible wounds in the wilderness battle. The colonel smuggled them and numerous other of their people here, but there was an accident.

Pearl's aunt was tossed about trying to land in a storm, and the baby in her arms was dropped into the dark water and drowned. Her aunt never recovered, and the baby had to be hurriedly buried while the family moved on to a safer destination."

Pearl interrupted. "I's now feel firmly that da baby was buried in that there tunnel. My aunt never would leave her baby, so's she ran off into the hills. She's musta had gone completely crazy, I guess. My mother, her sister, insisted on stayin' to find her, and's da rest of the peoples moved on."

All of us sat in silent awe. We took deep breaths and welcomed the pause. We took in the connections drawn by this story that was now nearly exactly one century old. This strange anniversary only added to the mystery and celebration of our chance meeting.

Pearl went on. "My mammy tolt me once she's knew where her sister was and how she could hear's her cry in da night if'n she's got to just the right place in these here hills."

Jack glanced at me, and because I was getting better at reading these nonverbal cues, I asked a question.

"Pearl, how did your mother describe the crying?"

"Oh, 'twas awful screams sometimes but often them low moans. One account I's heard described it as a howl."

"Yes, the "Howling Hills Mystery", that newspaper clipping you gave me the other day. I shared it with Jack along with that other story I told you about my friend's fear and his phrase 'hag herbs howl.' I believe these are all connected, with the exception of the one about my father and his duster. That has become a stand-ing joke in my family. But what we have and are sharing here is no joke, and I am deeply moved to be here with all of you sharing."

I suddenly noticed Jack was unusually quiet and sitting back in his chair. I couldn't really tell, but he seemed a bit pale; then again, I've been worrying about his aging a lot lately. As I was about to speak to him, he leaned forward with his elbows on the table, fin-gering his now-empty glass. He breathed in another of his signa-ture deep breaths, let out a sigh, and began to speak.

"I guess I'm not getting as old and senile as I thought. This is all fitting in, and I have another puzzle piece to add. Can I share with you all?" He had everyone's approval and rapt attention as he went on. "I've been coming up here with Em since my daddy died and gave me the place. I guess we came up here first in the late forties after the war. Every once in a while, maybe only once a year or less, we'd hear this sound. We passed it off as resulting from any num-ber of things, including boat motors, strange birds, wild animals, and on and on. Ron here and I heard the sound not long ago, and sometimes I felt it was coming from the basement or the tunnel; I'd call it a moan or…what do you think, son?"

"Yes, a moan or a groan, like a deep, sad crying of grief."

Pearl and Jonas nodded at what we were saying; Pearl especially was still deeply emotional as Jack went on.

"Well, I had a strange dream the night after the kids left," Jack said. "I passed it off as just being weird, as dreams sometimes are, but now meeting you all…let me share. In the dream I heard the sound. I went to the basement door. I didn't have to open it because there was something or someone there. I couldn't see features, maybe because they had a cloak on with a hood. The person stood there, but I wasn't scared; I felt kind of calm. Then it—he or she or it—put out a hand, and I took it like to shake it. Then he or she or it put the other hand around mine and said thank you. That's it—'thank you'! Then it was gone, and I woke up. What I remember most was a warm, warm feeling afterward."

We all sat there kind of dumb and looked back and forth at one another.

Pearl spoke. "Mr. Jackson..."

"Just Jack, please."

"OK, Mr. Jack. You's has helped my family's spirits rest. I's believe my auntie can now rest with her baby 'cause of all da connections you's helped us make. And you, son." She touched my hand. "My Lord sho' blessed me today by you, too."

I sort of whispered, "No more moans. No more crying." As we sat quietly, I thought, "Maybe now it will be a peaceful thing. It could be the quiet caress of the waves on the beach or the breeze in the leaves. Maybe it's the peaceful message of the loon echoing over the evening quiet." We were all very still.

Jonas spoke up. "Yes, Mr. Jack, we's been given a great gift today. I's don't claim to understand how dem spirits combine and share, but I's do know for sure that you is my brother."

❧

# 24 - Summer's End

*How can it do it?*

*How can it close the curtain?*

*On our growing and showing,*

*On our finding truth maybe for certain.*

*Summer was ending, and more than that*

*I had a strange feel, maybe all in my hat.*

*Jack was going home, I on to school.*

*Lonesome yet together was our rule.*

*We decided to close by an unusual route,*

*Put pen to paper, write and love what came out.*

Summer was ending fast. Dave was preparing to leave the store early and start his new job. Life was moving on to a different stage for him.

I got my registration letter from the university along with the course catalog. I noted my class preferences for the year. I was encouraged by all the adventure of this summer to take another history course about the Civil War and postwar Reconstruction. I had promised Jonas and Pearl I'd come back and share all my findings with them. For me, too, life was moving on to a different stage.

As we prepared to close the store and end the summer, I felt a certain melancholy come over me. I had already turned my back on my hometown and had been away at the university for two years now. I had no contact with any of my high school friends except Dave. My classmates were all off making their own lives. Other classmates had new careers already, with one in nursing and another who had moved out of state. Another friend was married and living across the state. What stage was I off to? I didn't know, but I was excited to be on the ride.

I came crashing back to earth from all of that excitement when Jack asked me for the second year in a row to help him drag the shutters from the back shed and I found Jack was noticeably less able to help. I was fine with that and encouraged him to stay seated and "just be the boss." He liked that role but also fussed about not being able to help. It was a warm day, and after accomplishing our work, we retired to the shade of the porch and rested.

I had stopped several days earlier and left copies of the information I'd gotten from Jonas and Pearl about the "Howling Hills Mystery." I also shared the letter I wrote them about my experience with the "Hags House" as well as the newspaper clipping about the "Fruit Farmer and His Howling Duster."

When I'd met with Jonas and Pearl, they were still all smiles about the visit to Jack and the discoveries of that day. Pearl was still feeling especially blessed and had said, "I's can't thank you enough for helping bring peace to ma peoples. There sho' has been a ton o' restlessness for years and years. My mammy was possessed by her worry over what happened to her sister and her inability to help. I 'member for years I a hearin' 'if I could only this' and 'maybe if I only did this or that'—all that worrying talk! I's believe she done worried herself to the grave. She's may well has become one of them restless spirits we's—and you, specifically—have helped to be released in peace. I's still feel a huge pressure has lifted and done flown away!"

Jonas added, "I think they's truly bound for glory now! Thank God for you and Mr. Jack!" Then he leaned in to me and winked. "My brother Jack!"

We had all been blessed. I had grown so much. How much I'd grown I'll never know, but even in my youth, I was smart enough to recognize the gifts these unlikely folk had given me by simply letting me into their lives.

When I returned to Jack's porch, I shared all this with Jack. He took on his usual sage look, lit his pipe, and slowly puffed some smoke. I expected it to encircle his head like a halo—not like a wreath but a halo. His only response to my long story was a guttural "humph" every once in a while. Finally, he reached forward and, sipping his tea intermittently, shared tenderly.

"I can't begin to tell you, son…we all learned a lot this summer. I'm still amazed at how much history you've found and pulled together about our own little River Clam. And then there's Jonas and Pearl—they're both just plain pearls if you ask me! And you know what else, son?"

"What?"

"They're black pearls, the most valuable kind!" He winked as he settled back in the chair.

He scratched a light again, and I saw the papers I'd given him earlier sitting on the stool by the window. They were under a Petoskey stone paperweight to keep them from blowing away.

"Did you get a chance to read these?" I picked them up and straightened them in my hands.

"You bet! But I tell you, you've been pushin' this here ol' brain awful hard to soak all of this in! Just so much an old guy can do. Now it's easy for you youngin's. Also, I'm depending on you to get this all in some order so others can learn just like us."

"What do you mean? You think I should write and publish a book someday?"

"Well, you got to do more than just write those fancy papers at the university! We've got more history and adventure going on right here than any of those folk you's studying! So why not a book?"

"Yikes, Jack! That scares me to death!"

"Oh, bah, it can't be that hard; just look at all the junk out there already published. Remember that book I shared about Cassopolis? That was written by a classmate of my daughter's who'd been a scientist at one of those chemical factories near Kalamazoo. He didn't know any more about writtin' a book than you. And you're still young. I think you should go for it! Maybe Millie can help. She works for the newspaper in Cass. Don't know rightly what she does, but I'm going to ask her when I see her tomorrow."

I immediately jerked out of my complacency. "Tomorrow? Millie's coming tomorrow?"

"Oh, don't get so ruffled. It happens every year, you know. We all get older, you included, and we just move on to other stages of our lives. The only guarantee we have is change!"

Jack figured we had rested and caught our breath long enough, so he came back to taking on his role as boss. First he had me deal with the stakes and wraps for the rose bushes. He didn't move from his old chair. He really got into that boss thing, pointing and shouting orders. I got a kick out of it and loved to be helpful. I moved the two planters off the porch. He wanted me to pull all the flowers this time, and I took them around back to his "brush heap," as he called it. Then he said he was worried about some chairs and toys the kids had left at the beach. So I checked it out and picked up some trash, a couple toys, and two folding chairs and stored them in the shed.

"We'd better do something with that makeshift fire pit!" he hollered.

"Do you want me to just put them back? I can see where some of them were along the path to the shed. Is that OK?"

"Nah! Put them all in a pile next to the shed, and I'll decide about it next..."

Jack got quiet. I sensed it was also sad for him to close up for the summer. He must have known his health wasn't good, and he had taught me all along to enjoy today because it was all I had. I think he was trying to do just that.

"There I go again worrying about Jack's health and what will happen next year," I thought to myself. I finished the rocks and looked around for other tasks to complete.

Jack called, "Come on up here, son. Enough is enough."

We settled back in the chairs. We split what was left of the iced tea. It was kind of warm now, so there was no ice left, but it was wet at least. I remembered the story Jonas and Pearl had shared about the rich lady who came to their house during the storm. Jonas had said, "Almost any ice melts sometime!" He was referring to the lady's icy personality that finally melted and she shared her food with the group. Maybe that was a good analogy for our summer together: The ice was melted; there no more barriers—just friends.

I sat in the quietness pondering that heavy thought. I noticed Jack had closed his eyes. I didn't know if he was napping, but I began to consider quietly leaving. The sun was low, and the breeze was soft and gentle. Actually, I felt like I could just stay like this forever. "Forever?" I thought. That wasn't possible because time marches on through stages, and as Jack had said, there were no guarantees except change.

About then, I glanced at Jack again and prepared to make my quiet exit. He was looking at me, not with any particular expression but just with those sage eyes that pierced my soul again and again.

"I've got an idea," he said. "Let's write a poem!"

"Together?" I responded.

"Sure, why not? I've never done that before. Have you?"

"No!" I smiled at the idea and said, "Yeah, why not?" I retrieved my writing pad from my backpack and handed it to Jack.

Jack looked at me with a startled look. "So you want me to start?" I started to say something, but he quickly came back with "And don't give me any of that 'age before beauty' stuff either!"

We both chuckled. He took the pen, thought for a moment, and wrote:

I feel like I'm watching another sunset.

I know it's mine, but I'm not there yet.

Handing it back to me, he said, "There's a start for us!"

I read it and frowned a bit. I didn't like the idea very much. I guess it was too real. So after thinking for a couple of moments, I wrote

I don't like sunsets for some reason now.

Seems odd. I'm feeling more sunrises on my bow.

Without comment and hardly any hesitation, Jack put his pen to the task and wrote

A ship and a journey are good images to keep.

Jump on the ship! Go afar before you sleep!

When I got the pad and the pen back, I realized how much my thinking this summer was about journeys, or water and rivers specifically. I'd thought a lot about our River Clam, so I added

I've often thought a river is also good.

I claim our Clam, and thankful here we've both stood.

Jack read and peeked over the top at me; those eyes twinkled. He looked out at the lake and back toward the river and then added his next line:

Standing together near opposite ends of a line

Yet celebrating together the meaning of time.

I could feel my insides start to tense and my emotions swell. I took a deep breath and even stopped for a sip before I wrote

I've learned from the sage a patience and view

Of life, time, and love which I never knew.

Jack read quickly and stopped to retrieve his handkerchief. He didn't seem to blow his nose so much as wipe those glistening eyes. Again he looked straight to me, in me, and through me, smiled, and penned

Be careful of sages! Fear not your own road!

Write your story yourself, yet carry one another's load!

He handed me the pad again. I read his last two lines and then reread the whole thing. I think my glistening eyes may have given it away! I couldn't continue to write anymore. I just held the pad and pen in my lap.

I looked at Jack; he smiled and patted my arm as he settled back in his chair. He closed his eyes. I began to feel scared. "Maybe I should shake him or something?" I thought. Then he spoke up.

"Let's not write anymore. That will give us something to do at another time."

I was glad he spoke up, for my tongue was tied, and I cherished the words he had written. I felt tears welling up, but I said, "Yes, next time, same place, next summer."

I reflected with a deep eerie sadness. "Next summer?" I thought to myself. "It feels so distant and far away."

❧

# 25 - Christmas Gift?

*What do you want for Christmas?*

*Would it be this thing or that?*

*For me it would be to return*

*To that favorite Clam River flat.*

*There find the sage, the pipe*

*The loon, the one-eyed cat.*

*The dread? Oh, from where?*

*From leaving home, but yet to there*

*Or here, I just don't get the future.*

*I'm going back. Or forward?*

*I just feel dread in the picture.*

Fall term was exciting. I'd joined a group planning a remedial teaching program in conjunction with a Negro college in the south. I was excited and looking forward to sharing that with Jonas and Pearl. Still, after finals were over and I was packing, a kind of dread came over me. I couldn't seem to shake it and tried to explain it away in a couple of ways.

I knew my home was here at school now. I lived with some guys in a house. We were all going different directions but at the same time learning to share the basic tasks of living together. We had to keep the place clean, take care of our own things, and share the cooking responsibilities. I was feeling completely on my own and there was an emptiness about going home for Christmas. I had all kinds of mixed-up feelings rattling in my head and gut. Were those part of my dread?

I had no connections to my hometown. I was looking at an empty two weeks away from friends. I couldn't even think of any girls who might be around to ask for a date. That was certainly a cause for dread.

I packed up my stuff. I was careful to include the research I'd done in the post–Civil War course I had taken. It was a small seminar-type class, and all we did was research, bring information back to the class, and present it to the others. The best part was that we would then lead a discussion on whatever topic we presented. It was very stimulating. I gathered tons of stuff Jonas and Pearl would want to see, including some documented maps of Underground Rail routes. We found that some of the trails did go through our northern Michigan area. That was more common than we'd earlier thought..

I was off down the road. Was I going back home? That wasn't quite accurate, but at least I'd be spending some time with my folks. That'd be worth the trip. I hoped I could find that Cassopolis address and drop Jack a Christmas card. That was enough for dread, I decided; it was Christmas! I loved Christmas usually, but this one seemed different.

I had offered to drop a friend off in Traverse City, so I came toward my folks' house from the south. I would usually have come up the middle of the state and come across from Mancelona. Coming

up through Traverse and on up along Torch through Alden meant I
would drive past The Clam.

As I rolled over the big bridge—the new one that replaced the
old swing bridge—I took a deep breath to relax. I was beginning to
feel a long way from school and final exams. I inhaled deeply and
let out a long, healthy sigh. I slowed the car and decided to turn
down toward the store for an old-time look. Immediately I hit the
brakes and skidded to a stop in front of Jack's place. I was in shock,
and I sat there for a moment with the car running. I felt numb.
Jack's cottage had a for-sale sign in the yard.

Looking around I noticed a couple other changes. The crooked
mailbox was gone. The bigger sign that said *The ack* that we had
joked about for so long was also gone. I got a sick feeling in my gut.

I drove on over to Dan's Bar, but it was the middle of the week;
it was only open on weekends. Heck, he may have been closed up
for the winter already. I hit the gas, spun a U-turn, and headed for
my folks' house. My mind was a blur of thoughts, plans, and partial
solutions, but mostly I was feeling just plain ol' dread.

No one was home when I got there. Again, it was the middle of
the day and the middle of the week, so they were both working. My
mom's school wouldn't have Christmas break for a week or so, and
my dad had just started a new job in Traverse City.

"Just as well," I sighed to myself. I got out my suitcase and some
stuff on hangers from the car. I found the "hidden key" there hanging in plain sight like it always had. My dad always joked, "A real
crook would just kick in the door or break the glass and open it. No
one but people who needed to would use a key, so put it in plain sight."
That didn't seem to me to be bad logic, and I chuckled out loud.

I staggered up the steps to the kitchen with my big load; I was too lazy to make two trips. I knew my mom wouldn't be happy if I tracked snow all the way in, so I struggled to kick off my boots, again with my hands full. Then I went through the house and put the stuff in the spare bedroom in the back.

They called it my bedroom, but again I never lived in this house except in the summer. There were a few of my things sitting around, but this just did not seem like my home or my room now. I was sure it was equally hard for my parents to adjust.

I wandered back through the kitchen, scoping around to see, pretty much as I had expected, that nothing had changed. I figured I'd go get another load of stuff, like the Christmas gifts I had brought. I stopped when I saw a note on the table addressed to me and written by my dad. I turned it toward me on the table and read *You got a call from Bob, the realtor, last week. It's about your friend Jack.*

Now I was confused. I hadn't seen Bob more than once or twice since he'd graduated four years ago. I had heard he was working for a realtor now. How would he know I was a friend of Jack's? "Too much thinking," I scolded myself. I grabbed my folks' phone and dialed the number on the note.

It rang and rang with no answer. Instinctively, I looked up his parents' number and decided to call them. His sweet mother answered on the first ring and acknowledged that she did indeed remember me. "You and Bobby were in high school together and played football together," she said. I hoped I was not being rude, but I shortened the reminiscing and asked her for Bob's personal number. She shared that he had recently moved into his own apartment with a girl whose name I did not recall. I thanked her and promised I would indeed pass on a hi to both my parents.

I called the number she gave me, and it rang only a couple times before he answered. I recognized his voice immediately even though he answered with an official-sounding "Hello, this is Bob from the Valley Realty. Can I help you?" I didn't even recognize the name of the realty company—things change quickly, especially when you're away. I explained I'd just gotten to my folks' house and was anxious to get his information. He said I should meet him at his office, gave me the directions, and hung up.

There were two cars there when I arrived, and I hoped one was his. I went in; I didn't know the lady at the front desk. However, Bob came out of his office as soon as I spoke, and there was no need for long introductions.

"Come in here," he said as he directed me into his small, cluttered office. Actually, it was a room about three feet larger on all sides than the desk. It seemed to me that he hadn't risen to the "executive suite" yet, and I smiled at my sarcastic thought.

"Here it is." He handed me a sheet of paper. I turned it toward me and read the name and the address with a phone number. The last name didn't register, but the first name was Millie, so I guessed it to be Jack's daughter. Before I could question, Bob spoke.

"Here, sit for a minute, and I'll fill you in on all that I know. I just made contact with this woman right before Thanksgiving. That was what? I guess it was only two weeks ago, if my memory works right. She had contacted Rolly's because they winterize and watch the place for her in the winter. Rolly told her to call me when they asked for a realtor recommendation. I must remember to thank them." Bob rummaged around, seeming to look for a paper on which to write a note.

"Please keep going. I am greatly concerned."

"Well, you know all I know now!"

"But it's for sale! Why?"

"Because they listed it!"

"I realize all that, but why?"

He shrugged his shoulders. "You must know more about this family, certainly, than I do!"

I settled back in the chair, and my mind flitted through a fast rewind of my wonderful times with Jack. "Yes, I guess I do."

With that I jumped up. I grabbed his hand and offered a quick thank you before excusing myself. I was out the door quickly and expect I left them both with their mouths open—I should have apologized for my hasty departure. I mentally noted that I had to do that later. Now I wanted to get home to the phone and make this call.

Back at my parents' house, still no one home, I sat at the phone to make the call. Digging the paper out of my coat pocket, I quickly dialed the number. I could feel my heart beating quickly. Then a woman's voice answered.

"Millie? This is Ron, from Clam."

There was quiet, and I heard her let out a sigh.

"Ron, I am glad you called, and I apologize. I had lost your number and couldn't get to you. I'll get straight to the point; Jack died in October. We all miss him terribly, but be assured he was peaceful. He just didn't wake up from his nap one afternoon here in his favorite chair."

She hesitated, maybe waiting for me to respond. Then she spoke up again. "Ron? Are you still there? Are you OK?"

I was definitely stunned but not shocked, because it was not like I hadn't already worried about this very news. I sighed hard.

"I'll miss him, too." That was about all I could say as I was starting to choke up.

Millie spoke up quickly. "Ron, give me your address. I need to send you the funeral brochure. I think you'll be glad to see it."

I was puzzled by her comment and couldn't imagine anything I could "be glad of." I gave her my folks' address. She assured me she'd be in touch soon. We hung up.

I just sat for a while. "So that was the dread I had felt," I commented to myself. I was glad I was alone. I wandered about lost, unpacked my stuff, and sat down. As I sat in the living room chair, I scanned the books in the bookshelf behind me. My eyes fell on *Whitman's Poems*. I smiled at the memory from two summers ago and pulled it out. Somehow it opened right up to where we'd marked it at "When Lilacs Last in Dooryard Bloom'd."

I read down, and I noticed it was blurring more as I read. I got to the line and breathed, "...drooping star in the west, and thought of him I love." I couldn't read anymore, and the tears just flowed.

On Friday a manila envelope came addressed to me. I had had nothing much to do, so I was home when I saw the mailman stop at the box. I threw on a coat, walked down, and got the mail. I ripped open the envelope as I walked up the drive. There was a letter and a folded program with Jack's picture on the front. It was snowing, so I didn't want to get it wet. I gently returned it to the envelope. I hurried anxiously back into the house.

I sat at the kitchen table and reopened the envelope. I read the letter first:

Dearest Ron,

("Wow!" I thought. "No one had ever addressed me like that except one girlfriend who I was no longer hearing from.")

You'll never know what a blessing you were in the last couple years of my father's life. When he returned this fall, he couldn't stop recalling all you and he had done, including with the Negro couple you had met. I'd love to meet them sometime.

Again be assured in your lonesomeness and loss that Jack is at peace. He just literally "went to sleep."

I wanted to tell you it was as if Jack knew what was happening. He talked to me and told me exactly what he wanted done at the funeral. Mostly he wanted the poem read and printed. You'll know what I mean when you open the funeral folder.

Ron, the poem was such a gift to all of us and his many friends. They were so touched that you and he had written what was your good-bye of sorts as well as a "thank you" for each other. He was a wise teacher, a wonderful father, and I hope a guiding friend to you.

Love,

Millie

I had to take a break and grabbed a tissue for my eyes. I gently took out the funeral folder. I lingered on Jack's picture. It had probably been taken in the last five years. He looked good. I could see the twinkling eyes and the sly grin. "God, I miss that," I thought.

I opened it and noticed the expected "Order of the Service." It indicated that they'd sang some songs and read some Bible verses. But then I noticed on the left flap inside was our poem—the poem we had written that last day before he left Clam. I read it. But then I got to where he had written the last line and I couldn't write anymore; he had added another line. Last summer Jack had written:

> Be careful of sages; fear not your own road.
> Write your story yourself; yet carry one another's load.

But then, below it, he had added a new ending:

> Friends come in all shapes and sizes,
> Show up in our lives in times unplanned.
> My life's been enriched, my horizons expanded.
> I'm thankful today for that one young man.

"Oh, Jack!" I muttered. I grabbed my pen and added my lines to
his:

> "Oh, Jack, my sage friend!
> Why must this be an end?
> I know you must go,
> But you'll always know
> We're a part of each other.
> That can never bend."

## THE END

# EPILOGUE FROM THE AUTHOR

While writing this story, I continued to struggle with "why". I think sometimes it might be selfishness. Other times I think it might serve the purpose of a memoir, a looking back. After all that over thinking, I have tended to return to the material I wrote in the introduction where I confirmed my life and my embracing of diversity. These are the reasons I wrote it. Yet I still continue to ask "So what? Why write about it, for no one really cares but me?"

An incident happened in April of this year that cemented my desires to write this story. I was doing some research to clarify some information. I got a reference from one of my contacts near Clam River and called an older gentleman in the area. He had lived there all his life and had become a sort of self-proclaimed "town historian." Maybe he was the only one with any memory left, but it did not matter; I needed some information verified.

I asked if he remembered the late-fifties storm, and he quickly replied that he did. I asked also if he remembered the family that had helped those stranded during that storm. He responded, "Why, yes, it was ol' Nigger Joe." I winced at his answer.

I went further and asked if he remembered their last name, and he replied, "Well, no. We just called him Nigger Joe. That's what we all did, and that is what he wanted us to call him." After thanking him and hanging up, I was deeply saddened.

I pondered as to what was making me most sad:

A. That the word *nigger* was still being used so easily in 2011?

B. That they never knew the man's last name?

C. That he, Jonas, played along so as not to ruffle feathers or cause a conflict?

D. That a person would have to do such a thing just to survive?

E. That our ancestors, our kin, were so callous as to think it was OK and it was what "they wanted"?

F. That nearly fifty years after I graduated from high school in the area, this attitude still persisted?

G. Or that I was still so innocent as to think the world had changed?

So I write for me! I write to apologize to Jonas. I said these words in Chapter 18, and it sums up why I write:

> So how does it end?
> Guess it's up to you and me!
> There was never a news report
> Written or shared for the world to see
> And get a glimpse of a miracle that had shown

That night in the swirl of the snow and the wind that was blown,
But there was still more happened there,
In the breaking of barriers, the peek over the wall,
Giving hope, maybe one day, we'll be able to love one and all.

Epilogue Thoughts: RCR

# Appendix A:

## <u>Alternative Chapter 19 as a Poem</u>

### The Storm

"The winds did blow, and then came snow."
When I came home, I had to write.
It was a lot to remember, so I wrote into the night.
I'd written my notes as soon as I'd gone.
Hope I got it straight,
Won't leave anything out or get anything wrong.
The story is told here because
They wouldn't tell it then
Because they were simply cowardly men.
Listen, and I'll tell you a story that's true
About a family and heroics few people knew.

## <u>PART 1: THE STORMY NIGHT</u>

I'll tell you a story that's true,
I hope you'll see better what all went through.
The storm of fifty and eight snowed late and blew at an awful rate.

The road filled, and consequently the traffic it slowed.
None of us ever sets out to be stranded.
Several that night were greatly surprised
And deeply blessed with where they landed.
Landing first on a long, empty stretch in a flat spot,

Fear set in quickly when no others, no cars,
No lights were seen, not even a dot.
One man and his loved one lived along that road.
They were poor; they were segregated; 'twas a heavy load.
They were used to hard times, so the storm they did not fear.
They sat close to each other as it roared and darkness neared.
Missus then said, "There must be some in trouble!"
Mister said, "I'll go with the tractor," and he left on the double.
Time went by, and darkness came heavy;
The wind wouldn't let up.
She worried but began to fuss with some sup.
Was it the wind? Or a big thumping limb?
No! 'Twas the door! It must be him!
"Open up, dear! There's company here!
Got some lost cold souls
Needing some heat, food, and cover from the cold."
Missus replied with a worried, wide smile,
"Oh, it's not much, but do come in!
Be welcome! I've got water hot,
And the coffee will warm you. I'll put on another pot."
"How," she thought, "How, oh how did they find each other
Out in the dark, barren and blowing, such awful weather?"
I can only guess as I fill in the gaps.
I do know one thing: instant community among strangers was the form,
And they huddled together, sharing selves, keeping warm.
Jonas shared and fed the folk and fed the fire.

As the wind and snow whistled, they began soon to tire.
There wasn't much room for the group, seven in all,
But somehow room was made with even one in the hall.
Everyone was leery and unsure of what to do.
Jonas figured was first time most had been
Close to a Negro and that put some in a stew.
The mystery remains over the years.
All together, so different, but not there alone.
For barriers, jobs, backgrounds, and colors
In this place did not come out worth a hill of bones.
Who were they, this gathering lost in the snow?
Not sure I know all, but some I do know.
One was a trucker strong and burly as his rig,
But the rig in this snow for sure would not go.
Second, the couple, locals by name "only a mile from home,"
Reluctantly and shyly came: "Can't make it on our own!"
The young salesman was freezing in his wing tips and thin slacks.
"I would not have lasted" was all in his thoughts,
But welcome he was: "Come on in; excuse our lack."
Last was the lady found in her large car.
So frightened and freezing, yet wouldn't open her window but ajar.
"I don't want your help; you're not my kind!"
"Come along anyway, lady. The others won't mind!"
She hesitated, shivering, weighing her chances,
And then chose to climb out.
No one missed her scowls and side-glances. But who'd have thunk?
As she observed the cold mix of rescuers with disgust,
She insisted on grabbing a big bag from her trunk.
She held it so closely most of the night.
Then like ice also softens,
She opened her picnic, and all shared her off'in's!

## PART 2: THE NEXT DAY

The storm was still raging when daylight did break.
The coffee and meagers were shared.
With no relief in sight, each one did partake.
One told of his family and worried for he knew,
With a wife pregnant and sickly, she surely would stew.
The big burly trucker did also relate
He and his wife had four kids and would soon reunite
For he was sure the storm was soon to abate.
Jonas was the first one to venture forth.
They shoveled snow and more snow, but the wind had gone
north.
That helped, and by afternoon a loud rumble was heard,
And the group quickly did stir
With the hope of a rescue they were yet to observe.
They were right as they peered past the driveway not cleared.
A huge snowplow was passing; they looked, and they cheered.
All spirits were rising as Jonas started the tractor and brought
out the chain.
The men proceeded with shovels; retrieving vehicles was their aim.
Now came an uncomfortable part.
They'd been so close, shared the food, kept the fire,
But now—and how?—they must depart.
The guys shook and shook and shook one another's hands,
Not sure what to say. Bye was not a man's way!
The ladies were better but still stuck in their ways.
Could they hug? Why not? This was a new day.
The lady of means was the first to say,
"I speak for us all, can't thank you enough.
Without you and your home, we'd not be here today."
Tears were surely shed, as all finally left.

Jonas and his missus looked around.
They thought of the love that did them surround.
It gave a warm feeling from their heads to their feet,
With little food left and a whole back shed dismantled for heat!


## PART 3: HAPPY ENDING OF SORTS

The winter returned to normal; all seemed to forget.
No mention from locals; no calls did they get.
Then one day weeks later came a knock on the door.
When opened standing beaming was the truck driver from
before.
He smiled and introduced a man in a suit
Who was some big boss who thanked them.
Then he and the company gave them a check and more loot.
They stood there without words
When the roar of the truck was again heard.
It backed up the drive and unloaded
New boxes from which new appliances near exploded!
After a lot of "oh nos" and "you should nots"


And "these will surely dos",
The crew quickly changed out the old for the new.
Pictures were taken, grins and smiles abounded.
Then all drove away, and when none were around,
Jonas and the missus were there on their knees
Thanking the Almighty for gifts
And praying a blessing on all of them:
"Oh, God, please! Bless and keep all these folk from any great
harm.
We don't know the next part; we'll just rest in your arms."

No newspaper people came by for the news,
But the word spread around.
Many were pleased and smiled wide, but some were just blue.
Jonas shared with me later he had visitors one night.
They were not happy men, and he feared they might
Hurt him and the wife whom he'd hid 'hind the door.
"Don't get a big head or smart mouth!" to Jonas they
deplored.
"You know your place and your kind,
Know what to expect, so don't get in a bind!"

So how does it end?
Guess it's up to you and me!
There was never a news report
Written or shared for the world to see
And get a glimpse of a miracle that had shown
That night in the swirl of the snow and the wind that was
blown,
But there was still more happened there
In the breaking of barriers, the peek over the wall,
Giving hope, maybe one day, we'll be able to love one and all.

Made in the USA
Charleston, SC
16 February 2014